IATEFL

31st International Annual Conference
Brighton, April 1997

Edited by Peter Grundy

Editorial Committee: Simon Greenall, Andy Hopkins, Caroline Moore, Cristina Whitecross

iatefl

Published by IATEFL, 3 Kingsdown Chambers,
Kingsdown Park, Whitstable, Kent CT5 2DJ

First published 1997

British Library Cataloguing in Publication Data
Education
Grundy, Peter (Ed.)
IATEFL 1997 Brighton Conference Selections

ISBN 1 901 09550 9

For a complete list of IATEFL publications, please
write to the above address.

IATEFL Publications Officer: Andy Hopkins. Copy edited by Sue Harmes.

Designed and typeset by Mike Brain, Oxford. Printed and bound in the EC.

CONTENTS

4 The new technologies

5 Language and language teaching

6 Conference reviews

EDITOR'S INTRODUCTION

You will notice that this year's *Conference Selections* look different from the *Conference Reports* of previous years. Most obviously, we have abandoned the A4 size and introduced a more professional, bookshelf-friendly format. This is part of **IATEFL**'s publishing initiative which aims to produce good-looking, high quality publications whose readership extends beyond our paid-up membership. My efforts as editor have been directed to trying to produce a publication which members, and non-members, really want to read and learn from. Most important is the quality of papers and reports, which this year is very high: many of them make a real contribution to developing the profession and deserve to be influential. All repay careful reading.

One criticism of previous *Reports* was their lack of overall coherence – an inevitable consequence of publishing over a hundred 250-word reports of presentations. This year, the limit was raised to 500 words and would-be report writers were asked to specify (and thus think carefully about) the area in which they were making a contribution to the profession. We have also abandoned the former practice of publishing the plenaries in one section and the presenters' reports in another. The six sections this year contain plenaries and presenters' reports alongside one another in what I hope is a coherent order.

One consequence of doubling the word limit for reports is that we were not able to include all the summaries which were submitted and so had to introduce a review process. Each report was independently evaluated by two members of the editorial committee and myself. The review process was 'blind', i.e. we did not know the authors' identities. It was amazing how rarely we came to different conclusions.

What then were the reviewers looking for? Because **IATEFL** is a professional organisation, we favoured clearly written papers which addressed professional rather than academic or research issues. We hope this policy will ensure that any washback effect these *Selections* may have is positive, and that the best conference presentations will continue to be those which address practical professional issues in a creative, effective way. One problem though: many of the most interesting presentations at **IATEFL** conferences are by authors reporting their new work. However, we have not included reports which we felt transgressed the boundary between descriptions of good practice and sales pitch.

The *Selections* contain the six plenary addresses, each limited to a maximum of 4,000 words, and three 1,000-word conference reviews commissioned from overseas members. 148 presenters sent in reports. 46 are included in full. In addition, 41 briefer extracts from reports which we could not include in full for reasons of space appear at the end of the sections which address their themes. We have called these 'shorts'. I regret that we couldn't include more, and would like to thank everyone who took the trouble to send in a report, whether included here or not.

The *Selections* are divided into six sections which reflect the distinct areas addressed by contributors. I suppose these are the areas of the moment in 1997 – in 1998 they may well be different. The sections vary in length, largely because some include plenaries and others don't.

The first section on methodology addresses the 'what', 'how' and 'why' of language teaching. It opens with Claire Kramsch's paper *In another tongue* in which she argues that we should work on the boundary between the forms and varieties of learners and their communities and those of the standard. Kramsch believes that learners should be encouraged to express themselves in mixed codes. Written from the perspective of the 'multiculturally inclined language teacher' who views 'other' as part of self, her paper is a fascinating blend of postmodern perspective and practical advice. This section also includes Rex King's description of the highly innovative Hong Kong public examination assessment of English, which has as one of its aims the promotion of washback effects which contribute positively to effective teaching and learning.

The second section focuses on teacher training and development – the 'who' of language teaching. It opens with Penny Ur's paper *Are teachers born or made?* Ur believes that the characteristic qualities of effective teachers can be learnt and that development is important even in initial teacher training. She argues that experience and openness often make those with fewer instinctive teacher qualities into better teachers than those to whom teaching comes most naturally at the outset.

The third and fourth sections focus on materials, classroom practice, and technology, the 'with what' of language teaching. As several reports addressed the language learning opportunities provided by the Internet and multimedia applications, section four deals only with contemporary technology. There are no plenaries in these two sections.

The fifth section focuses on language itself. Maybe it's a sign of the times that this year there are so many contributions on language, including three plenaries. The plenaries implicitly raise the difficult issue of how language knowledge should determine teacher education, student attitudes, learner materials and classroom activities. Jean Aitchison draws attention to prescriptivism and how learners are inescapably surrounded by gobbledygook, euphemism, and informal terms. She discusses some of the complexities of verb sub-categorisation and draws attention to the bleaching that often results from collocations and co-occurrences. Reading Aitchison's paper, we see how much implicit knowledge we have, and are forced to think of the position of our learners – how are they to learn about language?

In *Credibility gap? – The language we teach and the language we use*, Della Summers draws attention to the features of language that corpora highlight and which are inadequately represented in coursebooks: fillers, vogue words, tag questions, ellipsis, overstatement. She discusses the preference for agreement, the use of language to maintain solidarity, the role of implicit knowledge in conversation, and the way dictionaries represent these features of spoken language. Michael Hoey demonstrates the nature of cohesion in texts, and argues that lexical cohesion can be the basis for work on texts in the language learning classroom.

The sixth and last section consists of three conference reviews written by Guo Jieke, who works in China, Rama Mathew, who works in India, and Janaina Cardoso, who works in Brazil. Many of our members, especially those who work far from Britain, are not able to attend the conference. Who better to try and convey the dominant issues and the atmosphere of the conference than fellow overseas members who are able to attend? I'd like to thank our three reviewers for being the discriminating eyes and ears of those who couldn't get to the conference, for relating the conference to a non-European work context, and for informing members whose experience is restricted to UK and Europe of the wider context of ELT practice. In particular, these reviews provide an overview of dominant themes which does not emerge from reading the papers and reports submitted for the *Selections*. For Guo the conference was lexical approach, testing, and computers; for Mathew, testing, and action research for teachers; for Cardoso, professional exchange, learner independence, new practice.

The changes in this year's *Conference Selections* are experimental. I hope members and other readers will let us know which are positive, which we should re-think, and which we should have thought of but didn't.

Finally, I'd like to thank Simon Greenall for giving me the opportunity to edit these *Selections*, which has been a challenge and a pleasure. I'd also like to thank Andy Hopkins and Cristina Whitecross for their very conscientious work as reviewers. But most of all, thank you to everyone who sent in the papers and reports which I had the good fortune to read – thank you especially for your cooperation and unfailing courtesy under provocation.

Peter Grundy
University of Durham
July 1997

1 METHODOLOGY, LEARNERS AND PRACTICE

1.1 Plenary: In another tongue

Claire Kramsch, *UC Berkeley*

Hardly any other experience makes one more aware of oneself as both familiar and strange than speaking in a tongue different from one's own. Indeed, communicating in a foreign language has been seen recently by sociolinguistics and feminists as potentially constructing new social and cultural identities through encounters with the Other. What is the nature of this Otherness? What is the relation of language and cultural identity in language learning? In this paper, I look at various ways in which language learning methodology has dealt with 'the other' in the other tongue.

The cultural other as desired object

Colonialist views of language study: *appropriating* the linguistic other

In traditional language pedagogy, learning a foreign language in a classroom setting is viewed, like history, math, or other academic subjects, as the appropriation of a certain body of knowledge. Grammatical drills and translation exercises contrive to tame the unfamiliar and to piece together a social other in our image. A survey I conducted in 1987 of the 12 most popular German textbooks on the American market revealed how exercises to drill grammatical forms like prepositional compounds *dafür* (for it) and *dagegen* (against it), in fact were used to fight the East German other in the chapter on sports. Exercises like:

> Answer using *dafür* or *dagegen*:
> 'Sind Sie für die Demokratie?' (Are you for democracy?)
> – Ja, ...
> 'Sind Sie für Staatsamateure?' (Are you for state sponsored athletes?)
> – Nein, ...

constructed a German cultural reality that amazingly mirrored the American at the height of the Cold War. It did little to acquaint American learners of German with the real East German other (Kramsch, 1987).

In grammar-translation or in audiolingual methodologies, such practices leave their physical imprint. Students memorise rules of grammar, recite its paradigms, repeat its sounds, copy and recopy its texts. What becomes a body of knowledge is not in this case the lived encounter with the social other, but the literate encounter with the linguistic other. The language, spread out on the page in filled and blank spaces, in charted and uncharted territories, is, so to speak, free to be appropriated for the purpose of gaining access to the educated international elite. Latin and Greek used to be learned for that purpose in the old days; in many ways, English offers itself today as an instrument of colonisation, by giving its speakers access to international professional networks on the global market. Such strategies allow learners to keep clear of too close a contact with the foreign culture and society, while enjoying the benefits of a better education for having learned another tongue. Such an appropriation can have deep physical and emotional resonances for the learners. The desire to appropriate the other can often be the counter-aspect of a sentimental desire to assimilate to the other.

Assimilationist views of language study: *assimilating* to the other

For a large number of language learners around the world who are adolescents in classroom settings, the process of appropriation I have just described is often accompanied by an equally strong youthful desire to assimilate into the other. Language teachers, as representatives of educational institutions, might have to inculcate in their students the traditional values of these institutions, but many adolescents long to break out of the bonds of tradition. For these students, the foreign language might be a way out. Through necessity and peer pressure if they are immigrants to a new country, through romantic transference if they are yearning for new adventures in their home environment, the desire to shed one's old identity and to identify with the other, to become 'one of them', to act, talk, think like them, is often a strong incentive to learn the new language, especially if it is a high prestige language like English.

Viewing the other as a desired object is not unproblematic for a language learner. You may get your *r* straight and your idiomatic expressions right, but you may still never be accepted as 'one of them', not because of who you are, but because of what you represent. Livia Polanyi (1997) describes the travails of American women on a junior year abroad program in St. Petersburg who rarely got to become serious conversational partners in Russian, despite their appropriate use of the language, because they were invariably labelled 'females' by the dominant male segment of the student population and therefore free for the catch. It was in their best interest not to show that they knew too much Russian! Bonnie Peirce (1996) tells of Hispanic women immigrants to Canada who could not make their complaints heard by native speakers, despite their perfectly comprehensible use of English. Even if they were prepared to speak English like native speakers, they were not prepared to act as the helpless immigrants native speakers expected them to be. Even though they spoke native, they refused to think native. Meryl Siegal (1997) adds yet another obstacle to those for whom the other is an object of desire. Studying five Western women learners of Japanese in Japan, she realised that the Japanese were not at all keen on these foreigners becoming one of them. On the contrary: part of learning Japanese in Japan was learning how to speak and act like a Japanese-speaking foreigner, like a *gaijin*, not like a native Japanese – a sobering experience for any learner with a sentimental or romantic bent!

Such experiences have reinforced the views of those who have long claimed that the main purpose of learning a foreign language is less to colonise the other or to be assimilated to the other than to find and enrich oneself. These views come in two kinds.

The self as the discovered subject

The other as no different from self

One view holds that learning about the other is really learning about yourself inhabiting another tongue. The main purpose of language study is to enable learners to express themselves and their world but using other words.

Methodologies based on these views were in part born from the personal psychology of the sixties, in part from a linguistic analogy with children learning their mother tongue.

Personal psychology generated such humanistic language teaching methods as Curran's *Counseling-Learning Approach*. It capitalised on the perceived need of learners to express their own particular meanings in the here-and-now of the communicative situation. The learners whispered what they wanted to say in their mother tongue and the counselor just replaced their words by the foreign words – different labels for the familiar furniture of the universe (Kramsch and McConnell-Ginet, 1992).

Issued from psycholinguistic research in first language acquisition, Terrell and Krashen's *Natural Approach* strives, as we know, to reduce the gap between self and other and to minimise as much as possible the threat of the unfamiliar. *Natural Approach* textbooks for teaching French, German or Spanish in the United States, for example, choose situations and topics familiar to American learners: food, shopping, cars, sports, equal opportunity, the role of women in society. They avoid topics such as regional, national, and international politics, ethnic strife, or religion that would be controversial for Americans even though they might be of interest to native speakers of the language.

The other as another potential aspect of self

Besides these views from psychology and psycholinguistics that see the other as fundamentally similar to oneself, there have been recently other researchers' voices coming to the fore, this time from sociolinguistics, that see the other as another potential aspect of the self.

In a recent article, Bonnie Peirce showed how learners gain self-confidence and personal strength from the multiple identities they discovered in themselves in the process of learning the foreign language (Peirce, 1995). For example, Martina, a Czech immigrant to Canada, discovered that her social identity as a mother gave her the strength to deal with the discrimination she encountered as a non-English speaker. It enabled her, writes Peirce, to 'reframe the power relations between herself and the legitimate speakers of English' and to hold her ground with her landlord, her manager and her co-workers despite her insufficient grammar.

In her recent book, *The Linguistic Individual* (1996), Barbara Johnstone rehabilitates the individual speaker as the focus of sociolinguistic inquiry. Drawing on her research on language variation within individuals, in particular the speech patterns of women public figures in Texas, and invoking Bakhtin's notion of heteroglossia, and LePage and Tabouret-Keller's research on multilingual communities in Central and South America, Johnstone focuses on the many resources that people draw on when they live at multiple linguistic boundaries. For her, the use of one language over another is not so much an appropriation of someone else's language, nor an attempt to be someone else, but a matter of 'languaging yourself in another tongue', to use Pete Becker's phrase.

The view of the other in language learning as another dimension of the self is a seductive one. It is favored by cosmopolitans, travellers, and multiculturally inclined language teachers, among whom I count myself. Trish Sullivan and I have found it supported by the way English is learned in countries with strong oral traditions such as Vietnam, where language play and linguistic mischief can make the classroom into a pleasurable communal experience (Kramsch and Sullivan, 1996). It is certainly supported by work done in psychoanalytic and feminist theory (Kramsch and von Hoene, 1995; von Hoene, 1996).

The danger is that this self-enhancement or 'empowerment' of the subject, to use a trendy term, might not be as far reaching as expected, because it is not accompanied by an awareness of cultural difference and an exploration of this difference. Self-enhancement often creates value conflicts. When a Chinese man speaks English, does he just speak another variety of self, or does he not, rather, speak the language of identifiable Westerners who may have quite different world views and values from his own? And how is he heard both by Anglos around the world and by his Chinese parents, aunts and uncles? How is a Turkish female learner of English viewed by the religious elders of her Turkish family: as adding a religious dimension to herself, or, as is more probably the case, as gaining a suspiciously secular dimension? And are the two compatible? The learning of English around the world might accentuate, as it does in the US, the gap between the older, sedentary generation who speak the local language variety, and the potentially (hopefully upwardly) mobile younger generation who master the international idiom.

What we need to look at, then, is the very boundary between Self and Other and what happens at the border.

Life on the boundary

What does 'life on the boundary' look like, to borrow the title of Mike Rose's best-seller – a symbolic boundary, to be sure, the symbolic conflict that can occur whenever one discourse world encounters another discourse world? Two scenarios offer themselves: confrontation or mutual enrichment. I want to examine each of these options with some concrete examples.

Confrontation: Standard English vs Black Vernacular English – the Ebonics controversy

The recent 'Ebonics' controversy in the United States dramatically illustrates the symbolic confrontation of self and other in language learning. Last December 18, 1996, the Oakland School Board of the Oakland Unified School District in California issued a resolution that officially recognised:

> the existence, and the cultural and historic bases of West and Niger-Congo African Language Systems, and each language as the predominantly primary language of African American students.

It further resolved that:

> the best possible academic program be devised and implemented for imparting instruction to African American students in their primary language for the combined purposes of maintaining the legitimacy and richness of such language, whether it is known as 'Ebonics', 'African Language Systems', 'Pan-African Communication Behaviors', or other description, and to facilitate their acquisition and mastery of English language skills. (Cited in Fillmore, 1997:14.)

How did it come to such an extraordinary resolution?

The student population in the Oakland Unified School District is 53% African American. For a large number of these students, Standard English is, for all practical purposes, a foreign language. They call their home language Black English or Plain English, a variety of English which is different from the Standard Variety in phonology, lexis, grammar, prosody and general discourse features. However, unlike their Hispanic, Asian, or Filipino counterparts who are mandated by law to receive ESL or even bilingual instruction if their home language is not English, many Black students who have difficulties with Standard English are placed in 'special education' programs. In fact, 69% of all special ed. students are African Americans, the majority of whom are variously classified as 'learning disabled' (62%) or 'speech impaired' (15%). Hence the well-intentioned resolution by the Oakland School Board that caused such a brouhaha last December declaring that these children's difficulties were not, in most cases, due to any mental or physical disability, but rather to their lack of knowledge of this – for them – foreign language: Standard English. The language they came to school with, they said, was not a flawed version of White English, but another, perfectly respectable tongue, namely Black Vernacular English, to which they gave the name 'Ebonics', a 1970s combination of Ebony and Phonics (Fillmore, 1997).

The fierce debate that ensued regarding whether BVE is an African language, a dialect of English, or another language in its own right, that sparked the eloquence of my linguistic colleagues around the country, and that went right up to the floor of the United States Senate (!) missed the crucial point, as anthropologist John Ogbu was quick to show. For many Black children, the use of Standard English, while instrumentally endorsed as the language of social mobility and economic success, is at the same time violently rejected as the symbol of White Anglo domination (Ogbu, 1997). It is easy to understand the dilemma in which Black children find themselves in a White educational system where Blacks and Whites hold incompatible beliefs about the symbolic value of 'proper English'. By the way, the Standard English Proficiency Program set up in 1981 to train Oakland school teachers to teach Standard English has had a notoriously hard time defining what exactly constitutes 'Standard English Proficiency' beyond standard pronunciation, spelling and grammar (Schorr, 1997). This comes as no surprise, given the extraordinary variety of patterns of directness or indirectness, pace and rhythm, spoken vs written style, conversational features, and verbal creativity among the native speakers of English in the United States.

The case of Black Vernacular English is quite different, you may say, from that of foreign languages taught around the world. And yet ... the negative symbolic value of a foreign language is exponentially enhanced when the majority of its learners are viewed as belonging to an ethnic group whose cultural, political, or religious beliefs are rejected by the members of the target culture. The obvious need to become bilingual and bicultural must be supported by a recognition of the validity of the students' native language if acquisition of the other language is to be successful.

Mutual enrichment: Exploiting the transitional surfaces

Foreign language teachers around the world encounter more modest but no less visible symbolic stress between self and other in their day-to-day classroom practice. I want to explore how these tensions can be exploited rather than avoided. Each of the practices I mention attempts to put self and other explicitly into relation with each other.

Good teaching practice in recent years has tried to establish a meaningful link between the foreign and the self by stressing the embodied, physical dimensions of language use. Activities for self-expression like storytelling, jazz chants, reader's theater, creative writing have been part and parcel of communicative language teaching. However, these activities have generally been viewed as means of self-enhancement, not as a way of exploring the boundary and the potential non-comparability of self and other.

Recent suggestions have been made for having such creative language experiences focus more explicitly on the crossing from one language to another. In Kramsch and Crocker 1985, I suggested guided peer observation and comparative analysis of conversational interactions in one language and in the other to enhance the traditional communicative pair or group activity. Henry Widdowson's reflexive rewriting of poems (1992) and Paul Simpson's reflexive pastiches or rewrites of short stories (1997) further highlight boundary phenomena. Similarly, as I describe in Kramsch 1995, 1996 and 1997, critical group reflection on students' summaries of a common short story can provide the necessary awareness of linguistic and cultural boundaries.

With the need to ground the language learning experience in the physical dimensions of spoken and written style comes a renewed interest in code-switching of all kinds as a way of highlighting the relation between self and other. What some young researchers are advocating now is not a return to the disembodied translations of yesteryear, nor to the unbridled use of the mother tongue in the classroom, but a principled way of exploiting the potential pleasure of cruising the transitional surfaces between the multiple languages that learners bring with them to the classroom. Carl Blyth (1995) for instance, teaching French at the University of Louisiana, reports such cruising activities in his French class where speakers of Cajun French, French French, Cajun English, and Standard English are allowed to use their respective language varieties. His students describe their sense of gratification caused by the creation in the classroom of a 'multilingual speech community'. Julie Belz (1997), teaching German at UC Berkeley, makes systematic use of private journal writing to encourage her students to write multilingual texts. These journals have yielded unexpected insights into the pleasures of language-crossing as experienced by learners when they are given a chance to consciously choose which language they wish to use for which portions of their journal entries. Here is, for example, the journal entry of a 22-year-old Spanish-speaking beginning learner of German:

> A year, only a year later, waren wir so much verliebt, daß we were verlobt.

Not only does this multilingual text remain faithful to the syntactic rules of each language (German word order in 'waren wir', English word order in 'we were'), but the student is obviously sensitive to the particular meaning achieved by the juxtaposition of the two languages. The two German words *verliebt* (in love) and *verlobt* (engaged) bear not only phonetic similarity, but also semantic proximity, which, as the student herself explains, is for her the source of a little aesthetic epiphany:

> – I thought it was so cool because it's like almost the same word. It has different meanings and it's just the vowel ... At first I was going to write it ... in English but 'engaged' you know 'engaged' it just didn't it didn't go you know and so I looked for the word in German and I realized the match and I thought it was so cool that I just left it that way and I really love it. It's just the two vowels here and that one vowel there and that's the only change in the whole word.

She continues:

> La verdad es que no se como ni cuando, aber dieser Mann hat in meinem Herz einen Platz gefunden.
> – Some of the code-switching was either because it fit on the page or the structure. This part in German sounded better than in English or Spanish 'Dieser Mann hat in meinem Herz (sic) einen Platz gefunden' um it has this you know because of the verb at the end it just has this beauty in it. Not just the words themselves but the structure the way it's set up but in Spanish it would be so plain well the part *corazon* would be romantic, but the rest?

As teachers we tend to forget how beautiful even such dry linguistic features as German lexical roots or German word order may be for our beginning students. Fixated on the functional value of phrases and gambits, we tend to overlook their physical and emotional resonances.

The experiments described above are not meant to suggest that we should turn our classes into towers of Babel, nor return to the days of grammar translation. Rather, they show what pleasure students can draw from exploring the boundaries between languages and discourse features. This pleasure is derived from viewing the foreign language not as a monolithic self-enclosed cultural entity that one either appropriates or is assimilated into, but as a relational construct. The English language is different, feels different when spoken or written by a French speaker or by a speaker of Turkish. When learned by non-English speakers, English acquires a social, historical dimension that enters into contact with the historical dimension of the learners and of their country's history. English becomes relative, and it is the room for maneuver afforded by this relativity that gives the learners pleasure and self-fulfillment (Chambers, 1991).

Conclusion

In our attempt to define the relation between the self and the other in the learning of another tongue, we have passed in review several ways in which foreign language learning has been seen as an attempt either to colonise the other or to assimilate to it, to domesticate it or to find alternative dimensions of oneself in it. These different approaches have considered the other to be either a purely linguistic entity, or a social and cultural construct, or a psychological and aesthetic dimension of self. All these attempts have often had as their intended result to narrow the gap or even blur the boundary between self and other.

By contrast, recent attempts at defining the place of the learner vis-à-vis the other suggest that we focus now on the boundary itself. Teachers are called upon to teach to the boundary, not beyond it. Students discover pleasure at exploring the crossing, analysing the difference, testing the permeability and the irreducibility of the border. And so we might end up with the paradoxical insight, that in an age of global markets and worldwide information systems, language teachers teach foreign languages, not in order to eliminate linguistic boundaries, but in order to make them more visible and more appreciated.

References

Belz, Julie (1997) Language use as an index of the self-in-transition: Evidence from written multilingual texts. Paper presented at the *Annual Conference of the American Association for Applied Linguistics*, Orlando, FLA March 1997

Blyth, Carl (1995) Redefining the boundaries of language use: The foreign language classroom as a multilingual speech community. In Claire Kramsch (Ed.) *Redefining the Boundaries of Language Study* Boston: Heinle and Heinle, 145–84

Chambers, Ross (1991) *Room for Maneuver. Reading the Oppositional in Narrative* Chicago: U. of Chicago Press

Fillmore, Charles (1997) A linguist looks at the Ebonics debate *TESOL Matters. Applied Linguistics Forum* 17:1, 13–16

Johnstone, Barbara (1996) *The Linguistic Individual. Self-Expression in Language and Linguistics* Oxford: Oxford University Press

Kramsch, Claire (1987) Foreign Language Textbooks' Construction of Foreign Reality *Canadian Modern Language Review* 95–119

Kramsch, Claire (1995) Rhetorical models of understanding. In Thomas Miller (Ed.) *Functional Approaches to Written Texts: Classroom Applications. TESOL France* 2:2 Paris: USIS 61–78

Kramsch, Claire (1996) Stylistic choice and cultural awareness. In Lothar Bredella and W Delanoy (Eds.) *Challenges of Literary Texts in the Foreign Language Classroom* Tübingen: Gunter Narr 162–84

Kramsch, Claire (1997) Social discursive constructions of self in L2 learning. Paper presented at the Vygotsky symposium at the *AILA Congress* August 1997

Kramsch, Claire & Ellen Crocker (1985) *Reden, Mitreden, Dazwischenreden. Managing Conversations in German* Boston: Heinle and Heinle

Kramsch, Claire & Sally McConnell-Ginet (1991) Introduction *Text and Context. Cross-Disciplinary Perspectives on Language Study* Lexington, MA: D C Heath

Kramsch, Claire & Patricia Sullivan (1996) Appropriate pedagogy *ELT Journal* 50:3, 199–212

Kramsch, Claire & Linda von Hoene (1995) The dialogic emergence of difference: Feminist explorations in foreign language learning and teaching. In Donna Stanton and Abby Stewart (Eds.) *Feminisms in the Academy* Ann Arbor, MI: University of Michigan Press 330–55

Ogbu, John (1997) Beyond language. Paper presented at *The Ebonics Controversy* panel at UC Berkeley

Peirce, Bonny Norton (1995) Social identity, investment, and language learning *TESOL Quarterly* 29:1, 9–32

Polanyi, Livia (1997) Social categories and the construction of the foreign language learner. Unpublished ms.

Schorr, Jonathan (1997) Language panel aims at teachers. English issues still simmering *San Francisco Chronicle* March 23, 1997

Siegal, Meryl (1997) Learning how to be the 'other' (*gaijin*). Discursive practices and second language learning in Japan. Unpublished ms.

Simpson, Paul (1997) *Language through Literature* London: Routledge

von Hoene, Linda (1996) Subjects-in-Process: Rethinking Foreign Language Study through Psychoanalytic, Feminist, and Postcolonial Theory. In Claire Kramsch (Ed.) *Redefining the Boundaries of Language Study* Boston: Heinle and Heinle

Widdowson, Henry G (1992) *Practical Stylistics* Oxford: Oxford University Press

1.2 Translation and cultural learning

Monika Seidl, *University of Vienna*

My main concern in this workshop was how to promote cultural learning in monolingual classes taught by a non-native teacher of English who shares her students' mother tongue. I wanted to show how transfer exercises as well as source language comparison can help sharpen students' awareness of culturally induced differences as well as similarities between source and target language. I argued that translation exercises need not be strictly text-bound with a formal focus on code rather than on discourse. When translation exercises are confined to word-for-word translations, the line of words tends to become more important than the line of thought, which results in basically correct translations that do not seem to be right on the pragmatic level. What has been neglected in these translations is the cultural background, the situation each text is embedded in. Any focus on the cultural aspect of a text naturally leads to a new form of activity, which I called transfer of meaning from one language community into the other.

When talking about culture I am not thinking of culture as one holistic system, but culture as patterns of shared ideas and values. What I have in mind are dominant cultural patterns, such as free enterprise, liberalism or gender roles, which are basically shared in Western European countries.

Dominant cultural patterns also include all those big moments in a culture's or country's history that symbolise a country's unity and that over the decades have turned into the stuff stories are made of. The stuff a nation's dreams is made of does not easily cross borders. So this is an area where transfer activities will naturally play a crucial role.

As the object of study I presented press adverts. Experience has shown that students find press adverts most stimulating. Adverts often work in extremely subtle ways, and can reveal a lot about the audiences at which they are aimed and about the ideas and values supposedly shared by the people being addressed. This holds true for the simple reason that advertisements often try to sell products not with reference to their inherent properties, those of a watch for example, but in terms of images that connect the product to something. These images very often correspond to the dominant cultural patterns that are of interest to us.

Another advantage of press adverts lies in the fact that they may help us avoid typical pitfalls of teaching culture. We tend to spend an awful lot of time on discussing the problems of minority groups. What we easily forget, however, is analysing mainstream culture. As language proficiency is a matter not only of grammatical but also of cultural competence, a focal point of culture studies must be the dominant belief system that helps to determine people's uses of language. Furthermore, students in culture classes are normally bombarded with large amounts of sociological or political information, ranging from facts and figures to the subject of politics and institutions. Important as these facts are, we could aim at textualising as much information input as we can. One way of doing this is transfer exercises. In this way non-native teachers teaching in monolingual classes could exploit the circumstances they teach in.

The examples chosen were two Rolex adverts, one aimed at a male audience, the other at a female, which we used to work on gender roles. Next came a Budweiser advert featuring highlights of American history, which was used for transfer activities. The final examples were two Audi adverts, one created for the American market, the other for the German.

1.3 Anguish to empowerment – teaching reading for academic literacy at a South African university

Charlyn Dyers, *University of the Western Cape*

I teach academic literacy at the University of the Western Cape, South Africa. Our course is aimed mainly at first year ESL students from almost every faculty on campus and focuses on the acquisition of English and the study skills necessary in a university environment. For the past few years, lecturers on the course have been experimenting with a range of approaches to reading in an attempt to accord this area the same weighting as that given to writing.

'Questions with no right answers'
We learned this from John Rouse of Rutgers University (*Provocations* National Council of Teachers, Urbana: Illinois 1994). These questions focus on an emotional response to text – how the text makes the student feel, what memories are aroused by the text, which sentences are interesting and confusing, what they think the text is all about and whether they would recommend it to another student. While we find this method effective in the early weeks of the course when the students are battling to find their feet in the confusing academic environment, we feel that a mere personal response to a text is too superficial to take the students very far with their reading.

Academic reading skills
Skills like prediction, skimming, scanning, annotation and evaluation are essential in an academic environment where so much reading has to be done very fast. The concern is that the focus here is perhaps too much on extensive rather than intensive reading, so that this formal and cognitive response to text also only takes the students part of the way.

Uncovering the power relations in a text
We have drawn on the work of critical linguistics theorist Hillary Janks (*To Catch a Wake-up* Unpub. Diss., University of the Witwatersrand) in order to develop questions that provoke a critical response to text – questions to uncover the point of view of the writer, the use of persuasive and emotive language, whether the text is fact, opinion, truth or propaganda, and who has the power to speak in a text. This critical response to text is crucial at university, but can only be achieved when students fully understand the text.

Reading journals and logs
We encourage students to do extensive reading in their own time and to record this in journals. We also ask them to log how their reading of academic texts is improving through the application of academic reading strategies like SQ3R (Survey, Question, Read, Review and Recall).

Student-generated criteria for more effective reading
A lecture by Peter Winograd on the importance of helping students to reflect on their own work inspired me to ask my students to write letters to each other in which they explained what they did before, during and after reading a text. The students needed time to reflect on, and discuss their approaches to reading, and found this self-reflection to be a very important part of the activity. This class

activity generated a checklist of criteria for more effective reading which has become part of our course material. Students have also written to each other about their individual difficulties with reading academic texts, and the responses of their classmates to these difficulties have given us another list of student-generated problems and solutions.

We have responded to the 'anguish' our students say they experience when reading academic texts by teaching academic reading skills in a much more systematic way, and asking our students to keep the reading logs referred to above. The response has been most encouraging – more than 90% of them reported a dramatic improvement in their reading, as well as greater interest in wider reading for enjoyment.

1.4 Language learning strategies

Rita S Y Berry, *University of Exeter*

Recent research in the field of second language acquisition has highlighted the active nature of the process of learning a language. Learners are not passive recipients of knowledge. Instead, they employ strategies to go about their learning. This paper explains the meaning of language learning strategies and reports some of the findings of a recent investigation into language learning strategies.

What are language learning strategies?

Language learning strategies are the measures, either observable or unobservable, employed by learners in an attempt to increase their knowledge of the target language. They can be used to obtain information, enhance memory or produce the language. In addition, they involve the ability to assess the learning situation, plan and select appropriate measures to deal with problems encountered, monitor the learning processes, and evaluate the effectiveness of the measures employed in order to make any necessary adjustments in their use.

There are a number of different categorisations of language learning strategies. O'Malley and Chamot (*Learning Strategies in Second Language Acquisition* CUP 1990) classify strategies into three main categories: *metacognitive*, *cognitive*, and *socioaffective*. Oxford (*Language Learning Strategies: What Every Teacher Should Know* Heinle & Heinle 1990), on the other hand, groups strategies into two major categories: direct and indirect, which are further divided into six sub-categories: *memory*, *cognitive*, *compensation* (under the direct category) and *metacognitive*, *affective*, *social* (under the indirect category). Some researchers, such as Brown (*Principles of Language Learning and Teaching* Prentice Hall Regents 3rd ed. 1994) opt to draw a distinction between learning strategies (language input) and communication strategies (language output).

My research into language learning strategies

Subjects and methodology

The participants in my investigation were 20 Hong Kong Chinese secondary students studying in an independent school in the UK. Their level of English ranged from elementary to intermediate.

The method of enquiry was qualitative. There were three phases in the investigation: pilot studies, cross-sectional studies and longitudinal studies. The findings to be reported are based exclusively on the cross-sectional studies. In these studies, the participants were interviewed in depth to elicit the strategies they used in learning English in their school environment. Other methods, such as observation, student diary and written projects, were also used to assist the understanding of the students' strategy use. The data collected were analysed using Glaser and Strauss' *Constant Comparative Method of Qualitative Analysis*.

Findings and conclusion

65 types of strategies were identified and grouped into six main categories: *metacognitive*, *cognitive*, *memory*, *social*, *affective* and *communication*. It was found that many strategies can be put under the umbrellas of two or more categories. For example, a strategy can be both *metacognitive* and *social*; strategies can also be used in combination and in sequence; some strategies are overlapping.

Learning strategies are important because they help learners take control of their language learning and become more self-directed, resulting in improved language proficiency and greater self-confidence. They are useful for all learners, both the successful and the less successful, to enhance their language performance.

1.5 Learner independence as an alternative to classroom-based courses

Marion Geddes, *Project Scotland*

As a founder member of the **IATEFL** Learner Independence SIG I have long been interested in attempts to put the learner at the centre of the stage. What got me going was my increasing frustration with the inefficiency of so much classroom learning. Eventually I set up my own English language and teacher training centre, *Project Scotland*, in my home in the West Highlands of Scotland.

Every course has a maximum of eight adult students, who usually stay for a period of two weeks. (Note that I did not want to abandon the group, which has important social, psychological and practical functions.) They live in our home and so are immersed in English all day every day. Unlike regular language courses, there is no timetable. Students are free to study when they wish, as much as they wish. They can also study where they want – in the study room, the garden, the living room. The community plays an important part in extending the 'classroom'. Students meet many local people, young and old, and join in local activities.

Learning to become independent: What are some of the underlying principles?

Aims

Learners should articulate their aims – short-term as well as long-term. At the beginning of every course I get each student to try to make explicit their short-term aims. Some of this is done with the whole group present, so that students can find out more about each other.

Resources

For aims to be realistic, learners need to know what resources are available to them. These include people in the house or living in the village as well as books and cassettes. With each student I draw a kind of mind map describing their initial programme of study and linking aims with resources and activities.

Learner training

Learners should know something about the nature of language learning. We discuss some of the things about language learning that have helped to inform my teaching, such as the usefulness of vivid associations to aid memory, fluency-accuracy, and much more.

Planning and self-discipline

Learners should learn to plan their study and appreciate the importance of self-discipline. Every student completes a daily record, which can also serve as a forward planner. Students often encourage each other to study – or to take a rest, an important component in the study plan.

Looking beyond the course

Learners should learn study skills and techniques that are useful now and will be useful when they are learning on their own without the support of a teacher. I also want students to use and learn about a wide range of commercial materials that they can use when working on their own – grammar books with answer keys, listening materials with transcripts, different types of dictionaries, simplified readers.

Evaluation

Learners should learn to review the work they have done and evaluate their progress. Redrawing the mind map drawn on Day One makes students aware how far they have come. The daily record helps retrospective self-evaluation. The students also have points for comparison when they repeat the same type of activity or take part in similar events (for example talking with the same person) at different points in the course.

Conclusion

Is *Project Scotland* a special case? Yes and no. I believe the principles I have outlined can be applied to any learning or teaching situation. The implementation may look very different, but this is only superficial. The guiding principles remain the same.

1.6 Stories within stories within stories

John Pollard, *Saudi Development and Training*

A story ...

The main, outer story, was about 12 young adult Saudis of the type we call 'damaged beginners'. They had studied English for three to six years in local schools, had graduated with poor results, were said to be unteachable, lacking motivation. Even a sympathetically designed proficiency assessment triggered very little communicative ability.

Around 300 hours of intensive classroom contact seemed to help them through an affective threshold and gain notable interactive oral proficiency. At the end of the programme they were videoed holding feedback interviews with teachers, although these formed no part of any assessment. With their permission I was able to show extracts from these videos at the conference, revealing communicative ability, structures, lexis, and strategies for learning and communicating which exceed the usual scope of published teaching materials which target content or context at this level.

... containing stories ...

The teaching programme referred to commenced using an intermediate L1 (Arabic) interpreter. The content was a focus on language and language learning, with reflections on past experiences inspiring classroom tasks which were non-threatening and fun, aroused critical self-examination of beliefs, and provided lots of instructional English input. The contact was spread over ten months, with short intensive classroom phases followed by periods of trying it out in the world.

A habit of sharing stories about individual language learning experiences began to develop. Sometimes these stories captured microlinguistic feats, as when Daifallah said 'uncareful'; sometimes they were extensive encounters outside the classroom, as when Fahad phoned and made an appointment with a teacher, or when Mussalam helped an Egyptian lady to complete her bank transaction by interpreting to the Indian counter-clerk who spoke no Arabic. The stories served to affirm the value of individual experiences (thereby increasing motivation and curiosity) and covered the complete range of narrative types recorded in casual conversation analysis (*anecdote*, *exemplum* and *recount*).

... containing stories.

The videoed discussions mentioned earlier were totally unplanned and unrehearsed, yet were sustained dialogues of around 30 minutes revealing no disabling communicative stress. The extracts presented at Brighton showed how the language learning stories were recycled from the world knowledge that learners and teachers had built together. They were referred to, partly or wholly retold at relevant points in the discussion, and used as reference points to introduce new episodes. They seemed to facilitate NS↔NS-like features of interaction, such as anticipating and completing each other's turns, interrupting to add relevant information, and segmenting for confirmation and clarification. Startling differences were evident between these and the initial proficiency interviews, where there had been no shared world and therefore very little language possibility.

Perhaps language learning stories could lend a thread of cohesion to any programme which allows teachers the time to talk with their students. For us they also provided individual, post-event evidence for *have done* descriptors of attainment, avoiding the deceit and damage of an everyman syllabus and standardised attainment tests.

1.7 Teaching Japanese students: Common problems and how to address them

Gillian Monk, *University of Portsmouth*

In this talk *problem* was defined as 'that which adversely affects the learning process in the classroom, and in particular, that which inhibits communicative interaction'.

The following were considered:

- problems in multi-cultural classes if Japanese students are placed according to overall multi-skill test results;
- classroom shock, especially different perceptions of teacher/student roles, methodology, class size, furniture arrangement, forms of address, etc.;
- the need to be aware of *tatamae* – polite smiling, nodding and agreement, i.e. giving the teacher the answer they are perceived as requiring; *omoiyari* – deferring to the other person in communicative interaction; *wa* – seeking harmony and avoiding conflict, which affects students' responses; silence – viewed as more important and conveying more than speech, contrasting with Europeans and Arabs who rush in to fill silence with words;
- the effect of place on Japanese sociolinguistic behaviour. The classroom is a silent place: the refectory is not. In my opinion, conversing with Japanese students and building relationships outside the classroom is crucial;
- politeness strategies. Scollon and Scollon (*Intercultural Communication: A Discourse Approach* Blackwell 1995) suggest that the teacher who favours a communicative approach fosters a low Power/Distance (PD) politeness strategy.

I suggested the following:

- the high PD politeness strategy found in Japanese EFL classrooms with a hierarchical, asymmetric base is transferred to the classroom in England;
- in the refectory, and other non-silent places, Japanese students use low PD, or perhaps low P/high D with foreign students and high P/low D with their teacher;
- Japanese students need to transfer low PD from the refectory to the communicative classroom to interact effectively with the teacher and fellow students. Interaction between teacher and students outside the classroom will, hopefully, encourage this;
- role-play enables students to interact in pairs or groups outside the student role and classroom situation;
- play reading (and drama in general) enables students to interact as the individuals in the play rather than themselves;
- using English first names: in Japan students are addressed by their family names, so adapting to a new English first name is not so difficult. From classroom observation it would appear that this releases the student from having to conform to Japanese sociolinguistic norms.

1.8 Ways with *Word* in teaching one-to-one

Valerie Bevan, *The Cambridge Centre for Languages, Sawston Hall*

A versatile word processing program makes it possible for the one-to-one student and his/her teacher to work collaboratively on a wide variety of text genres. Many of these are incorporated into *Microsoft Word 6.0* and *7.0* as templates. But the focus of this presentation was a type of text for which there can be no template: the transcript. I considered why transcription from a range of sources chosen to reflect the student's professional needs and personal interests is a useful exercise, comparing it with listening comprehension on the one hand, and traditional dictation and grammar dictation on the other. Observations of students doing transcription and samples of a variety of transcripts produced by learners from different L1 backgrounds were adduced as evidence of its value as a diagnostic tool for the teacher and an awareness-raising exercise for the student, and as a way of providing authentic language data that both student and teacher can put to other purposes.

Different ways in which teacher and student might work through early drafts of a transcript were suggested: the use of program functions such as text colour, for example, to prompt self-correction, to highlight lexical phrases, to group words with a significant feature in common (e.g. a vowel sound, despite different spellings) or to indicate which parts of a transcript could be used as a template for the student's own productions. The use of printed and recorded annotations and of ways in which teacher or student can signpost particular language points using the call-out function were also shown. I also drew attention to the ease with which language data collected in this way can be transferred to other exercises and information from other texts and reference works on computer can be incorporated into the language work on a transcript and personalised for the student. The presentation finally looked at the use of a complete transcript of a speech as the basis for a new speech prepared by a student for their own purposes.

Such detailed work in constructing or reconstructing, studying and manipulating a text is time-consuming for both student and teacher, and ideally suited to the one-to-one context. It may have many possible outcomes, but all of them constitute worthwhile, attractive components of the personal textbook which the one-to-one student and their teacher collaborate in compiling.

1.9 Beyond recipes

Tessa Woodward, *Pilgrims and Hilderstone College*

Recipes (short teaching/learning activities that are fully specified as to materials and time needed, aim, level, etc. so that they can be implemented fast and repeated easily) are extremely useful. They can be used at short notice, can be fitted around the edge of a teacher's own methodology, and can be used to test out class reactions to new ways of working. They are not one-offs since hundreds of variations can be created from one recipe. They can also, if overused without grounded principles, be rather bitty both to learn and to use.

Teachers are well-used to 'chunking up', using frameworks of a higher level of generality in which to store individual ideas or recipes. The 'pre-in-post' receptive skills model is one such good peg to hang collections of ideas on: whenever you meet a nice new idea that you could use before, during, or after a text or tape, it can be mentally absorbed into this framework.

If we think in terms of *categories of moves* rather than individual recipes, we move into a very generative area. I introduced the idea of stimulus based teaching here. The moves that can be applied to any stimulus under the sun (whether a verb list, a potato, a coloured page, a photo) are, in order, *encountering the stimulus, analysing it, personalising, alteration/ transformation, creation or empathy*. The categories of moves were explained, exemplified and tried out by participants. (See Woodward T & S Lindstromberg *Planning from Lesson to Lesson* Longman 1995.)

The next set of generalisable procedures introduced were those applicable to short texts. The categories here were *expansion, reduction, media transfer, matching, selection/ranking, comparison/contrast, reconstruction, reformulation, interpretation, creation, analysis, project work*. This time, participants worked through the categories of moves applying them to a one-sentence text. (See Maley A *Short and Sweet* Vols 1 & 2 Penguin 1993.)

There was time at the end of the session to discuss issues such as:

- whether it was advisable to do all the categories each time and in the same order (People thought not);
- whether some categories worked better with some classes, stimuli, teachers than others (People thought they did);
- whether the categories were really just catalysts for thinking and creating (Yes) and whether participants could come up with their own categories and generative frameworks (Oh yes! Definitely!).

1.10 Company, products and customer relations

Paul Emmerson, *International House Executive Centre, London*

Is there an elusive business communication skill that covers what business people do when they are not having a meeting, using the telephone, giving a presentation or socialising? It would need to account for such areas as discussing current projects, describing a process or system, talking about terms and conditions of sale, describing trends, dealing with complaints, discussing the company's products and markets, explaining what gives a company its competitive advantage and talking about the external business environment. Some of these topics are well-handled through a conventional approach of presenting and practising language, others are better dealt with through a student-led TTT (test-teach-test) approach, perhaps using frameworks to help structure the speaking activities.

In general, business English teaching tends to use a higher proportion of TTT because of its greater flexibility, its adaptability to the needs of individual students, the little time available on a typical course and the preference of business students for doing lots of speaking. TTT also lends itself to the idea of students simulating what they do in real life inside the classroom, a fundamental tenet of the business English approach. For these reasons, business English teachers are quite accustomed to giving input through feedback rather than at an earlier presentation stage, and need little convincing of Michael Lewis's telling comment that 'there's no problem with PPP, it's just that it takes two years not fifty minutes'.

However, the idea that TTT solves the problem of PPP is quite wrong. The transition from the second to the third T is just as problematic as the transition from the second to the third P. In fact it is the same problem. Many teachers ignore this, perhaps using the new idea of 'noticing' as their justification. According to this argument, feedback (the 'teach' in TTT) is basically awareness-raising. The student will move to production at their own pace, after noticing the language in the real world many times. Exactly when this happens is largely outside our control.

I argue that this approach is wrong, and that practice is also necessary as an aid to long-term noticing. In a PPP coursebook lesson, this point is obvious and we are right to expect that the author arranges practice activities. However in a student-led TTT lesson the point is far from obvious. The temptation is just to give feedback on a speaking activity and then fail to follow up the language points. But feedback, no matter how well the explanations are made, is presentation and not practice. In the talk, I suggested some simple activities for practising (manipulating) language that has come from the students and that we have already fed back on.

1.11 Communicative teacher talk

Richard Cullen, *Canterbury Christ Church College*

Studies into classroom discourse typically focus on the characteristics that make, or fail to make, the discourse 'communicative'. Criteria for communicativeness are taken from what is felt to constitute communicative behaviour in the world outside the classroom. Thus, Nunan suggests that:

> ... genuine communication is characterised by the uneven distribution of information, the negotiation of meaning (through, for example, clarification requests and confirmation checks), topic nomination and negotiation by more than one speaker, and the right of interlocutors to decide whether to contribute to an interaction or not ... In genuine communication, decisions about who says what to whom and when are up for grabs (Communicative language teaching: making it work, *ELTJ* 42.1 1987)

With regard to teacher talk, there are a number of characteristics which are frequently cited as being communicative in that they are felt to exhibit properties of genuine communication. One such characteristic, for example, is the use of *referential* questions, that is questions to which the teacher does not know the answer, as opposed to *display* questions, that is questions the teacher asks in order to test the students' knowledge. Conversely, there are other characteristics which are often considered to be 'anti-communicative' in that they are seldom, if ever, present in the social interactions between people outside the classroom. Examples of such features would be excessive, or exclusive, use of display questions by the teacher, the teacher's tendency to echo student responses, and to give feedback exclusively on the form rather than the content of what they say.

The problem with this analysis of teacher talk is that it attempts to set up criteria for communicativeness according to a model of interaction which operates outside the classroom, typically in small, informal, social gatherings, and is thus arguably inappropriate as a yardstick for assessing the quality of teacher talk in the context of the classroom – typically a large, formal gathering which comes together for pedagogical rather than social (or purely social) purposes. Furthermore, it risks setting up an unattainable and ultimately de-skilling model of classroom interaction for teachers to follow.

We need to consider what being communicative entails in the context of the classroom and of language learning, and not just in the context of social interaction outside the classroom. To do this, it would, I suggest, be more productive to define categories of teachers' verbal behaviour in a typical classroom, and attempt to determine what it means to be communicative in each one, as well as what would constitute a communicative balance of behaviours for teaching and learning purposes. Such categories of teacher talk would include questioning, responding to student contributions, presenting information, organising, evaluating and establishing and maintaining classroom rapport (cf. Bowers 1980, cited in Malamah-Thomas A *Classroom Interaction* OUP, 1987).

A model of communicative teacher talk should reflect its primary function – to support and enhance learning, and be judged by whether or not it does this effectively. Attempts to characterise communicativeness merely in terms of features of authentic communication which pertain outside the classroom are over-simplistic and ignore the reality of the classroom context and the features which make for effective communication within that context.

1.12 Courting the Law on University pre-sessional and in-sessional courses

Stella Smyth, *Leicester University*

This session outlined the legal writing skills which overseas Law students are required to master in the first year of their degree. These skills are linked to three types of tasks: the extended *argumentative essay* which is produced outside of timed conditions, the *discursive exam essay* in subjects like Contract, Tort, Constitutional Law, and the *problem essay* which requires a different format and approach to the writing task.

I suggested that a legal writing syllabus on the pre-sessional and in-sessional English for Law courses would impart both the macro and micro skills represented in these tasks, and that the teaching of them would parallel the stages at which the students need to know how to plan, organise, synthesise and present their views in one of these writing forms.

Students are not given a problem and list of statutory and case references to consult until about a month into the degree programme. The pre-sessional course therefore focuses on teaching the process of planning, researching and word-processing an argumentative essay approximately 2,000 words long. Given that the majority of the students have not yet studied Law, suggested titles would focus on current legal issues such as *Should there be a mandatory life sentence for murder?* The skills covered would include orientation to the Law Library and the compilation of a bibliography, note-taking techniques for extracting information from legal sources, summarising and reformulating facts and quotations, including footnotes, using objective language to express points of view, applying the conventions for writing an introduction and conclusion.

The modular in-sessional course would authenticate the writing experience further by selecting a problem from a previous exam paper once students had been taught the legal concepts and the terminology in which they are enshrined. The key differences between the approach to writing a *problem* and a *discursive* essay would be presented, building on what the students have already learned to distinguish about the discursive text. Features of the *problem essay* such as the set phraseology for dealing chronologically with the legal issues inherent in the problem, key phrases for referring to cases and statutes within the main body of the text, and methods of summarising the judgements to support arguments, would be made apparent in the form of authentic essay models, adapted to highlight a particular writing technique. For instance, students could be given an answer with beginning and ending included, but with information concerning the summary and application of legal principles omitted. They would brainstorm the legal issues orally then refer to the model and supply the missing information in the form of case summaries and legal opinions, while writing within the framework of the specific phrases for making legal cross-references and applying the law to the facts of the situation.

1.13 Shadow theatre and its appeal in the art of storytelling

Egon Turecek, *Pädagogische Akademie Ed Wien*

The workshop was divided into two parts and activities centred mainly around two different kinds of shadow theatre.

The first part of the presentation was devoted to shadow theatre with puppets. The story *The Mouse and the Apple*, in which five animals with varying degrees of patience are waiting for an apple to fall from the tree, was presented with cut-out figures moving behind a small screen. In the story *Frederick*, which was improvised by participants, special effects were achieved with colourful OHP transparencies.

The second part of the workshop focused on shadow theatre behind a big screen, a very expressive form of acting in which players convey actions and feelings through gestures and movements of the body. As a warm-up and icebreaker, participants moved to the sound of disco music. Two overhead projectors placed next to one another created attractive double shadows. Coloured cellophane and dimmers contributed to the atmosphere. Participants then worked on *The Magic Stone*, a story about a tramp who uses a cunning trick to get some food from a miserly old woman. He makes her believe that he can cook a delicious soup just from a stone. Gradually he gets the woman to bring him some onions, carrots, salt, and even a piece of meat to add to the flavour! All these props can be easily produced as they are just two-dimensional and simply cut out of cardboard.

Why is shadow theatre a suitable technique for young learners?

- the screen helps to reduce inhibitions, children can 'hide' behind it;
- the emphasis is on the auditory, visual, and kinaesthetic mode. Thus multi-sensory learning is achieved;
- tasks must be separated and therefore a relatively large number of children can participate: speakers, technicians, musicians, performers behind the screen;
- social learning is enhanced through the common goal;
- if you have a public performance in mind, for example you want to show parents what their offspring have achieved in the foreign language even after a few weeks of learning, great effect can be achieved with relatively little effort. The props are simple and inexpensive to produce.

On the whole, the workshop tried to establish that shadow theatre is a highly motivating tool for language learning. Moreover, it is fun and a feast for the eye!

1.14 Plenary: Can public examinations have a positive washback effect on classroom teaching?

Rex King

This article looks at the English Language question papers from the largest of Hong Kong's public examinations. These papers were designed to produce positive washback in the teaching and learning process.

Background

The Hong Kong Examinations Authority (HKEA) is responsible for two public examinations which are administered in the fifth and seventh years of the secondary school curriculum. The first of these two exams is called The Hong Kong Certificate of Education Examination (HKCEE) and it is taken by some 120,000 students who are mostly 17 years of age. The examination's main purpose is to decide who shall go on to sixth-form education. Those who enter the work-force at this juncture use it as an employment qualification.

HKCEE English Language

The current examination syllabus was examined for the first time in mid-1996 and, since the exam is the culmination of a two-year course, teaching for it commenced in September 1994. The new syllabus has four 'papers' designed as follows:

Paper/content		Syllabus weighting	Examining time
I	Writing	26%	1 hr 10 mins
II	Reading, comprehension & usage*	24%	1 hr 30 mins
III	Integrated listening, reading & writing	32%	1 hr 30 mins
IV	Oral	18%	c. 15 mins
* the objective paper: multiple choice items, gap filling, etc.			

Good washback as the leading design principle

Public examinations still dominate the teaching during the last four years of secondary education in Hong Kong. This gives rise to several exam axioms:

The HKEA axiom: If we don't examine it, it won't be taught.
The teacher axiom: If it isn't examined, I don't need to teach it.
The student axiom: If it isn't examined, I don't need to learn it.

The student axiom has certain corollaries:

Student corollary 1: If it is not in the exam syllabus and my teacher tries to teach it, I will object and make life miserable for him/her.
Student corollary 2: Since passing exams is my No. 1 goal, then anything and everything that helps me prepare for the exams must be good.
Student corollary 3: I should bully my teachers into teaching old exam papers and pseudo-exam papers.
Student corollary 4: I should spend my private study time cramming for the exam by doing/redoing old papers and pseudo-exam material.
Student corollary 5: If I can't persuade my teacher to cooperate in reaching these goals, then I will sign up with a tutorial school which has a 100% exam focus.

This is a somewhat flippant analysis of the attitudes of Hong Kong students and teachers towards examinations but, unfortunately, it does sum up the situation quite accurately.

Given this background, it is not surprising that throughout the 18-year history of the HKEA, all development work on English Language syllabuses has been aimed at improving the washback effect of the exam on classroom teaching. In other words, the aim has been to try to minimise the harm that excessive 'teaching to the test' can do. It has also been very difficult to persuade Hong Kong teachers and principals to accept the desirability of having an element of teacher assessment as part of the public exam process. Teachers see it as extra work and dislike the change in the teacher/student relationship involved. In addition, all sides worry about the integrity of teacher assessment. This has increased the pressure on the HKEA to find creative ways to test English in a realistic manner.

How can public examiners engender good washback?

The principles that the HKEA uses for designing and setting English Language question papers are as follows:

- we aim to narrow the gap between the language tasks set in the examination papers and the kind of tasks that will be faced by a Chinese speaker of English in the Hong Kong work/study environment;
- we do everything possible to maintain the reliability of the exam process, but in an environment where the highest priority is given to ensuring good face validity;
- we give priority to setting tasks which need the integration of a range of language skills on the grounds that this is a 'real-life' requirement;
- we test grammatical competence indirectly: i.e. in context and not in stand-alone, discreet point questions;
- in objective tests, we make extensive use of passages (of the cameo type) regardless of whether we are testing vocabulary, comprehension, grammar or syntactic/structural relationships;
- we define oral competence as being more than accurate pronunciation, good intonation and the ability to convey information accurately. We add the requirement of being able to function in a group by:
  - using appropriate interaction skills such as showing courtesy to others in the group
  - demonstrating turn-taking strategies such as avoiding domination and encouraging those who are shy
  - helping to reach a consensus/demonstrating problem-solving skills by knowing how to agree, disagree, give opinions, persuade, etc.

What kind of exam papers do these working principles produce?

1 Composition paper

In composition papers there has been little change during the past 18 years. Currently, there is an emphasis on making sure the students know the purpose for which they are writing. In other words, they are asked to play a role and they know the intended audience.

One traditional bad washback effect of examinations on writing compositions has been the practice of memorising model essays or 'seeding paragraphs' which can be inserted at appropriate places in the composition. This practice is strongly discouraged by the HKEA and dealt with harshly whenever it is detected. All 250–300 members of the HKCEE English Language composition marking panel are instructed to draw the attention of the chief examiner to any suspected memorisation (part or whole). These compositions are then put aside and looked at by the subject officer concerned and the chief examiner. If they agree that all/part of the work is not the student's own, it is crossed out and the composition is re-marked without the offending part. If the whole composition has been memorised, the candidate scores zero. This procedure is widely publicised. Candidates each receive an examination handbook after they register and it contains a clear warning on this point. A detailed examination subject report is publicised each year and the English Language reports always contain actual examples of memorised work. In this way, the matter is kept in the public eye and the incidence of this undesirable practice is now extremely low.

2 Objective paper

The HKEA uses objective papers (multiple choice, gap-filling, matching lists, etc.) with a certain degree of reluctance since, by their very nature, they tend to have a bad washback effect on both teaching and learning. They are used in Hong Kong mainly because of their value as monitoring devices to check the reliability of the scores in those papers which have a high level of subjectivity in the marking.

The way the multiple choice paper is used in the HKCEE is too complex a matter to be discussed here. However, it should be pointed out that there are ways to lessen the damage done by such papers in terms of their undesirable washback effect.

3 Integrated reading, listening and writing paper

In terms of integrating skills this is the most sophisticated English paper that the HKEA has produced to date. The candidates are required to come to the examination centres (280 halls and 1,700 classrooms) equipped with their own Walkman radios. The listening test is broadcast over one of the government radio stations.

The candidates are given a data file and a question/answer book. Part A involves doing a number of tasks in response to spoken statements, conversations and telephone calls. The tasks require such things as reading timetables, filling in order/application forms, interpreting maps/graphs etc.

Part B is the most interesting in terms of innovation. The candidates are required to listen to a 15-minute broadcast and to take notes while they do so. Before they begin, they prepare themselves by reading and/or listening to a description of the role they have to play. Then they have five minutes to look at the four tasks that are set out in the question/answer book. They are also encouraged to quickly scan the information in the data file to try to get a clearer picture of what they are listening for. After listening to the broadcast, they can complete the four tasks. This may involve using material from either the broadcast or the data file, but usually from both. It should be noted that much of the material contained in the broadcast and in the data file is not required – choosing what is relevant to the tasks is one of the important skills being tested.

4 Oral test

The oral test adheres to the principle that the candidates should play a clearly defined role. The aim is that this role should reflect real-life situations – so far as is reasonable within the constraints of a public examination setting.

In Part 1 of the oral test, the students play a role with the two examiners. They approach Examiner 1 to get information to fill in a form. Then they go to Examiner 2 who, without looking at what the candidate has written on the form, debriefs them as to the content it should contain. Both examiners award marks for content and fluency.

In Part 2 of the test, four students sit down together and form a four-person committee to discuss a practical task that they have had two minutes to consider. They are told very clearly what is expected of them and what the examiners will reward and penalise. This information is provided in a booklet called *Guidelines for Oral Candidates* which they have access to through their schools. They can purchase their own copies if they wish to.

How effective are the HKEA's washback measures?

This has to be looked at from two points of view, (a) what is taught and (b) how it is taught.

What is taught

From this point of view, the HKEA's measures are extremely effective. The influence on teaching content extends right down to the beginning of the secondary-school English Language curriculum, i.e. five years before the exam is sat. The changes that have been made to the examination syllabuses have had a profound effect: much more time is now devoted to both oral and aural skills and there is a much greater emphasis on the integration of skills. These changes are immediately obvious if one compares the content of the textbooks currently in use with those formerly used.

How it is taught

Despite the revolution that has taken place in terms of teaching content, teaching methodology has changed very little. Far too much time is still focused on the examination and its particular formats and far too little attention is given to the most efficient ways of acquiring the skills which the examination tests.

There is some evidence that some of the changes that the HKEA has made have produced some negative washback. One example comes from the changes to the oral examination. At least initially, many teachers have concluded that the new format is too daunting, and are convinced their students cannot cope.

Many of the weaker students take a similar view. The outcome has been that students, encouraged by their teachers, have resorted to memorising lists of set phrases to cope with most of the situations encountered in the oral tests. Hence they learn phrases that can be used to politely interrupt, to politely disagree, to change the subject, to encourage a shy person to enter the conversation, etc. This leads to very stilted conversation and can really get on the nerves of the oral examiners who hear the same phrases dozens of times in the course of an evening!

Even when teachers are personally convinced of the obvious truth that doing old exam papers or pseudo-exam papers is not the best way to ensure that their students do well in the exam, there is still the problem of convincing students and their parents that this is the case. Hong Kong students often take matters into their own hands by going in their thousands to tutorial schools where the focus is unrelentingly on the exam.

The Hong Kong experience can be summed up by saying that it has been comparatively easy to change the exam formats, the textbooks, and hence the content of what is taught in the classroom. However, it will take generations to change teaching methods because of the pressure students (and their parents) bring to bear on the teachers. Of course, it goes without saying, that teachers the world over find exams a useful 'stick' to motivate their students. As with corruption, there can be a 'satisfied customer' aspect involved.

Learning a second language is a slow business that requires a high level of personal discipline. To the individual learner, progress always seems imperceptible. Involving oneself with actual exam material seems a much more concrete way to proceed. How exhilarating to speed down the education highway at the rate of 60 multiple-choice questions per hour or one exam 'crammer' per week – surely that must be more effective than just reading more, listening more, speaking more and writing more!

1.15 Peer and self-assessment – optimising the acquisition of essay writing skills

Svetlana G Dimitrova, *Institute for Foreign Students, Sophia*

The study explores the view that validity of assessment of essay-writing can be enhanced by a closer correspondence between the way students think raters assess their writing and the scoring criteria raters actually use, assuming the latter are 'perfect' judges. It also suggests posterior-to-writing training in peer and self-assessment as a possible route for its achievement.

So far peer and self-assessment have mainly featured in the literature as a general learner strategy (Ellis & Sinclair, 1989) or as an indispensable part of the process of writing, bridging from the draft to the final copy of each and every individual attempt (Hedge, 1988; Brown & Hood, 1989; Smalley & Ruetten, 1990; White & Arndt, 1991). Scholars and teachers have assumed that students already possess adequate self-assessment skills, which, however, turns out not always to be the case.

In the experiment, both teachers and students were asked to judge a representative set of ten essays written by the same group of students using an undefined ten-point scale. In order to avoid the problems of uncertainty of assessment criteria, no instructions were given to either group apart from the information about the general expectations from the students' writing at this fairly advanced stage in their studies. This was felt to be justified because it was not so much the absolute value of the score itself as the correlation between the given scores that was of importance for the research. Comparison of judgements confirmed the hypothesis of the students' inability to self-assess their work adequately and meet their readers' requirements. A 'remedial' training course in self-assessment was designed, utilising Kelly's *Personal Construct Theory* (1955) and tailored to suit the specific needs of the class.

In accordance with this theory – and to raise the students' metalinguistic awareness of the language as well as to prompt their critical judgement – special attention was paid to the need to expose learners to a significant number of scripts representing various degrees of proficiency and key culture-specific problems found in their own writing. The first half of the course involved bottom-up, form focused work and the second half involved top-down, content focused considerations. The teaching method was predominantly collaborative group work involving revising the set of sample essays. Thus imperfections in the product of writing were made salient on the basis of comparison sufficiently informed through background and context, and possible sources of failure were detected in the face-saving situation of student-to-student and student-to-teacher conferencing and feedback. An empathising-with-the-teacher authentic attempt at essay scoring was regarded as an essential part of the training experience in assessment, so the students were asked to go back and re-assess the original set of essays upon the completion of each half of the course.

The experiment resulted in the gradual adjustment and finally in the expected correspondence in the scale scores between teachers and students. A new attempt at discursive essay writing showed significant improvement in the students' writing skills.

1.16 'Shorts'

Comparing learner and teacher views on classroom activities for EFL, *Matt Peacock, City University of Hong Kong*

The genesis of the research on which this session reported was the notion that differences between learner and teacher views on the usefulness and importance of various EFL activities can cause problems in class.

... All the studies had similar results: learners preferred more traditional activities, and teachers preferred communicative type activities.

... Results indicated the existence of a considerable mismatch between learner and teacher beliefs; in particular, learners rated error correction and grammar exercises much higher, and pairwork and groupwork much lower, than did the teachers.

Let's do business: The language of negotiating, *John Stephen Byrne, Abacus Communications, Dublin*

The author reported a number of findings, firstly, when learners at different levels of proficiency are grouped together, they generate more interactional adjustments than learners that are at the same level of proficiency. What this means in practice is that learners at different levels of proficiency may have to work harder to ensure that both parties understand each other clearly. It is argued that this 'adjustment-in-interaction' may be crucial in language development (Van Lier, 1988:162).

The second finding gives important feedback to the programme designer. Importantly, learners spent most of their time involved in transactional inquiry interactions, that is, asking questions, exchanging information and making sure that they understood each other clearly. You would want the questioning behaviour to show a high number of transactional inquiries. This would suggest that the learners are at the right level of proficiency and that they find the materials motivating. There was little evidence of procedural inquiry. This is very important. If there are a lot of procedural questions, it suggests that the programme is not very user friendly, that is, the instructions are not clear, the navigation path confusing. Likewise, there was little evidence of code enquiry. This suggests that the language in the task or used by the participants was not causing too much difficulty.

Finally, learners at the same level of proficiency generated more 'sustained' talk than mixed level pairings. Swain affirms that 'opportunities to produce sustained output in the second language are crucial to the second language learning process. "Sustained" talk provides the opportunities for variety and complexity of language use and it forces the learner to pay attention to how content is expressed.' (1983:237)

Homework notebook: A friend indeed, *J Banan Sadeghian, Allameh Tabataba'i University, Tehran*

A quick look at recent publications will prove that material designers conceptually and many even explicitly have arranged their 'presentations' as pre-, in-, and post-classroom activities. Practically, this has enabled foreign language teachers to expand their teaching time and consequently their learners' learning time.

... Fortunately, work on reflective and involved learning and teaching and the practice of keeping learning logs, diaries or journals has helped many teachers and their students alike to develop a very useful attitude towards homework and its involved and reflective implementation.

- Homework assignments need not be limited to post-classroom activities. They may be about future classes, including pre-learning and while learning activities.
- Teaching can be based on the homework assignments. They should be considered as learners' input.

Homework: Is it asking too much?
Elena Voyeykova

Homework – probably one of the least popular topics among ELT authors – can contribute significantly to learning a foreign language. It is an important form of self-instruction because it stimulates independence, responsibility and a creative attitude to learning.

We discussed a variety of home writing tasks, from highly teacher controlled ones, like doing drills, to minimally controlled ones, such as writing essays, in order to see how they affect learners' motivation. We believe that in many cases students' interest in the language increases with the growth of opportunities for self-expression and experimentation. Freer kinds of home tasks make learning more challenging and exciting. They also boost students' resourcefulness and confidence in what they are doing. Homework is a necessary part of the learning process because it helps students acquire skills for autonomous learning when they can self-direct and monitor their own progress.

... A survey on homework conducted by the author among her students showed that learners prefer less controlled kinds of home writing tasks. They enjoy taking the initiative and appreciate being given opportunities to work independently and creatively. Difficulties do not discourage them as long as they are willing to express themselves and are given a chance to do this.

Life beyond CELTA: Transition and development, *Ivor Timmis and Nigel Shaw, Leeds Metropolitan University*

Are we preaching the right things? Most of the evidence suggests that we are. However, there are clearly deficiencies which it may or may not be possible to address on a four-week course. Evidence for these deficiencies was that:

- there is a low take-up rate on pronunciation teaching
- many trainees are involved in teaching for which the course does not prepare them (e.g. 63% in one-to-one teaching, 43% in Business English, 47% teaching children)
- many trainees have to take responsibility for course planning from an early stage.

Dictogloss: A study of a collaborative means towards language development, *Alan Fortune and Dilys Thorp, Thames Valley University*

Dictogloss (hereafter DG), or grammar dictation (Wajnryb 1990), involves students taking notes from a text read aloud, and then attempting in groups to construct a text which has the same meaning as the original. It is not a traditional dictation activity. Students have to produce their own grammatically accurate text. Finally, each group's product is shown to the class on OHT, language points are highlighted and corrections made as a whole class activity. The Vygotskian view underlying this contextual approach to grammar is that collaborative text construction facilitates individual interlanguage development.

Our mutual interest in DG first arose through using Wajnryb (1990) for classroom group work, and intensified on observing the large amount of language and metalanguage use the activity engendered. We then encountered the work of Swain and Kowal (1994) who viewed DG as a collaborative venture in language awareness-raising and conducted research into Canadian second language learners of French doing DGs in pairs. They found evidence that in co-constructing a text learners 'notice the gap' between what they wish to say and are able to say, and provide useful feedback for one another in collaborating to solve linguistic difficulties. Our current project involves analysing audiotape recordings of our EFL learners doing DGs and videotapes of our class feedback sessions.

Skill-oriented pedagogy: Interpreting in China, *Jing Chen, University of Westminster and Xiamen University*

Interpreting involves understanding a speech event expressed in one language and producing another similar speech event using a different language and for a specific audience. The interpreter is a communicator who represents the author, but has a distinct responsibility towards the target language receivers. Based on this understanding, we have tried adopting a model of two-step operations in the interpreting class, namely the comprehension operation and the reformation operation, in order to reinforce the students' feeling that they are communicators with a communication responsibility.

EAP today: Exploring best practice, *Roberta Wedge, University of Westminster*

The lecturer I observed spent a great deal of class time clarifying the main assignment so that everyone knew what to do, acknowledging that some students are too shy to ask him about it in front of a large group. He asked occasional questions of the class at large, but did not pick on any student who seemed unsure or silent. He was willing to take questions from the floor at any point, especially on matters of clarity. All of these measures help non-native speakers and can be recommended to all teaching staff.

Assessing spoken English, *Alan Moller, Trinity College London*

The starting point is the assumption that the purpose of testing spoken English is to establish the extent to which learners can communicate effectively and accurately with other speakers of English (L1 and L2) in situations closely resembling those of real life.

My major preoccupations as an assessor can be summed up in two words *sample* and *assessment*. Will the sample of language generated be adequate for a valid assessment?

Listen first: The priority of language orality in communication, *Anna Rebuffo*

- The habit to listen, record, repeat after a model is basic and greatly supportive in the process of learning a language, especially at beginner level.
- Repetition is a supportive activity at beginner level and springs from listening: listening to peers' repetition provides students with a model.
- Students may correct their peers if they listen to them and get used to listening to themselves and correcting themselves, thereby becoming independent learners.

Training and developing teachers for teaching English for business, *Adrian Pilbeam and Christine Johnson, LTS Training and Consulting, Bath*

A Business English teacher has to know something about business, although we do not feel it is essential to have worked in business.

Business English is a kind of ESP, and needs analysis is therefore a key element. But even if teachers do not have to carry out a formal needs analysis themselves, they should at least be sensitive to the needs of their learners in terms of what approaches or what topics are preferred, or what kinds of language will be most useful.

EAP vocabulary learning strategies in a self-access centre, *Julia Hathaway, the American International University in London*

At Chengdu University of Science and Technology in China, we prepared postgraduate students to sit the IELTS prior to going to British universities to study or research. The students were mature, highly-motivated and already independent learners being researchers and often self-taught in English.

Success in the IELTS requires extensive reading, inferencing techniques and making appropriate selections of lexical items to learn. In contrast, our students believed in, for example, intensive reading, translating all words and visual memorisation of lists of vocabulary. During the first term of the programme, the teachers were in the position of imposing new procedures which the students largely rejected.

What about the older language learner?
(Poster presentation), *Barbara Fairburn*

Many of the difficulties associated with age appear to change in importance at different stages of life. Lack of time, pressure of work and family responsibilities appear to affect those in their 30s and 40s most, while those in their 60s and 70s are more concerned with problems they associate with memory and grasping new ideas. Beliefs about the negative effects of age on learning were common throughout all age groups, particularly as regards worsening memory, and these, together with fixed beliefs about the 'correct' way to learn languages sometimes appeared to place obstacles in the paths of older learners. A further difficulty for some was readjusting to academic study and to sitting at desks after many years in a completely different working environment.

Age does not however bring only negative experiences. The positive benefits of age include increased motivation, improved self confidence as regards talking to teachers and other learners, and the ability to relate new knowledge to past experience. Some teachers felt older adults were easier to work with and more likely to be more persistent and determined than younger learners. Attitudes to language classes were also more positive: as one student reported, 'It's more fun learning languages when you're older.'

Alternative approaches to literary texts,
Maria Raffaella Benvenuto, University of Jyväskyla, Finland

The actual activities that I have proposed do not always stop at response and may involve manipulation of the texts in question. For instance, changing the setting or modifying the characters of a well-known piece of literature is a kind of activity that is quite sure to appeal to teenagers, as the success of several Shakespeare adaptations for the big screen has recently demonstrated. Another activity may involve supplying alternative points of view, for example of characters that are mentioned in the text but not actually present, or providing reasons for a particular character's behaviour. Furthermore, the ubiquitous comprehension questions may be replaced by questions written by the students themselves to other students in the class which relate to the emotional content of the text they have read and concern individual reactions to feelings and situations.

English language needs of students in Hungarian technical universities,
(Poster presentation), *Csilla Sardi, University of Portsmouth*

1 Students felt that they needed more focus on vocational and academic English than was provided during language instruction.
2 Students wanted to concentrate on grammar, translation, speaking and understanding more than EFL teachers felt necessary.
3 A strong discrepancy was found between students' and EFL teachers' perceptions regarding the usefulness of different classroom activities. All in all, students seemed to rely on traditional techniques more than teachers did, although some modern methods (e.g. problem solving and role play) were more popular with students.
4 Students' level of English proficiency was not sufficient to fulfil employers' requirements in work situations.
5 EFL teachers assumed that students would use English more often for general purposes than for vocational and academic purposes, whereas the students thought the opposite.
6 Students appeared willing to use English for academic purposes more often than was required by subject lecturers and was expected by EFL teachers.
7 Employees needed English frequently for various purposes within the vocational domain and it was evident that such uses were not given the focus they deserved in EFL courses.

What Business English teachers need to know,
Steve Flinders, York Associates

Since York Associates was started in 1981, Business English has increasingly become an umbrella term for a wide range of related areas of training; and these developments are reflected in the various kinds of training we now offer. There is training to develop:

- language knowledge: people communicating internationally need both the structures of the language and the specialist vocabulary relating to their own particular jobs.
- communication skills: they need to be able to get their message across in writing, on the telephone, in meetings, in presentations and negotiations.
- intercultural skills: they need to communicate with people who may have very different expectations about the forms, the meanings and the settings within which communication takes place.
- professional context: they need knowledge of business – not traditionally something which the trainer had to provide, but now in emerging economies where a business culture is weakly rooted something which the Business English teacher may be expected to provide.
- management skills: as business becomes increasingly international, business people increasingly have to manage projects, build and lead teams and communicate with customers in English.

The *York Associates' Handbook* sets out to guide practising and would-be teachers through this potential labyrinth, to provide basic information in all these areas, and to point readers in the right direction towards developing their own skills and knowledge further on their own. It can thus serve as both a basic guide to read through, and as a reference book.

2 TEACHER TRAINING AND DEVELOPMENT

2.1 Plenary: Are teachers born or made?

Penny Ur, *Oranim School of Education, Haifa University*

The phrase 'a born teacher' is not usually meant to be taken literally. People who use it do not seriously mean that someone is born with a certain teaching DNA configuration in their genes. They are, rather, referring to stable personality characteristics, resulting from a combination of innate and environmental influences, that the teacher brings to their professional practice and that produce something that looks like a natural bent for teaching.

Is there such a thing?

What evidence do we have for the existence of 'born teachers'?

The existence of the phrase

First there is the actual existence of the phrase as an immediately recognisable collocation in English. Compare *born engineer* or *born scientist*. The mere fact that the expression is a recognisable cliché that slides easily off the tongue implies that the concept is popularly accepted and based on folk wisdom.

What the professionals say

But beyond folk wisdom, what do professionals think? I asked two groups of teachers, a group of 20 novices and a group of 25 experienced, competent professionals whether they thought there was such a thing, and if so whether they were themselves 'born teachers'. The inexperienced teachers were almost unanimously positive in their answers to both questions. The experienced teachers were more cautious, though still a majority (80%) thought there was indeed such a thing; but only 32% thought they were definitely born teachers themselves, 28% said they weren't and 40% were uncertain. So in general: yes, teachers think there is such a thing.

Research

A third piece of evidence in favour of there being some truth behind the expression 'a born teacher' is research. There is, of course, no research on the topic as such: researchers prefer to look at more quantifiable or at least observable phenomena. So I went to the literature on good, or expert, teaching, to see what I could find. Three factors other than 'born teacherness' have been discussed as potentially important contributors to good teaching: methodology; training; experience.

Methodology: It is almost impossible to prove that one method is superior to another through research, because of the immense number of other variables in any teaching situation. You cannot isolate methodology and say that it is the critical variable (Ellis, 1994). We can, however, reach some more useful conclusions about methodology if we approach the topic from the opposite point of view, trying to falsify rather than to prove: is there any evidence that methodology does **not** matter?

An interesting study of successful teaching (not ELT) in elementary schools in Colorado (Clarke, Davis, Rhodes & Baker, 1997) studied three outstandingly successful teachers, each of whom used an entirely different methodology. They were equally successful. The researchers did find various characteristics that these teachers had in common – but method was not one of them. This suggests that we may be able to discount the choice of a particular methodology as a critical variable in successful teaching.

Training: Most of the teachers I asked stated that their professional preparation courses were valuable. My informants came up with statements like 'My training courses refined my own ideas, gave them a reason (theory behind it) and put things that I guessed were there into a framework', and 'Without training, professional knowledge, you may remain ineffective and inefficient, even though you may have good rapport with the kids'. But even with the most effective training programmes, some trainees do not manage to learn; or they do well on the courses and then for some reason do not succeed in the classroom.

In another broader survey I asked several hundred teachers in Brazil what their major source of learning was. They answered almost unanimously that it was experience (Ur, 1996). Pre-service training scored fairly low, and in-service rather higher. But the same teachers also said that initial training had been very important for them, particularly at the beginning of their careers.

Experience: Many researchers have documented the difference in expertise between novice and experienced teachers and defined the ways in which this is expressed (Peterson & Comeaux, 1987; Richards, Li & Tang, 1995; Richards, 1997). The implication is that what matters is not what you are born with, but the amount of experience you have.

However, this does not account for the phenomenon of experienced teachers who are not expert: and they do exist. Bereiter and Scardamalia (1993) looked at the behaviour of experts and non-experts (not necessarily teachers) with similar periods of experience. They found that both had developed high degrees of automatisation of routines over the years and were able to do the same jobs far more quickly and efficiently than novices. The difference was that the experienced non-experts simply took less time on the job, and had more free time as a result; whereas the experts used the freed-up time to try out new ideas, develop further, and work out better procedures. So that time spent on the job, for the experts, never in fact got any less: it was, however, used more efficiently, with better results and constant personal progress.

Interim summary 1

Of the three factors I have looked at that contribute to the good teacher, methodology probably contributes very little; training is a significant but not decisive factor; experience (and reflection on it) are probably the most important single factors. But even experience does not account for everything: there are significant differences in the level of expertise of teachers with similar experience. We are left with *x*, some quality or qualities which cannot be accounted for by method, training or experience: 'born-teacherness'. Let us call this the *t*-factor.

T as a multiple intelligence

Through discussions with teachers, it has become clear to me that there is no one *t*-factor that makes for 'born-teacherness'; it is a kind of multiple intelligence, composed of a number of distinguishable, though sometimes overlapping, qualities.

We can, perhaps, distinguish further between general abilities that would make a person competent at a number of professions – medicine or counselling, for example, and specific teaching abilities.

General qualities
General qualities might include the following:

- content knowledge: the knowledge of the theory and practice of the relevant field of knowledge (Shulman, 1987);
- intelligence: in particular the ability to think rationally and creatively, to generalise from specifics and vice versa, to solve problems;
- inter-personal relationships: the ability to get on with people in general; tact, empathy, warmth;
- organisation: the ability to think systematically, to organise items in real time and space;
- responsibility: the ability and willingness to take on responsibility for people and processes;
- confidence: a good self-image and belief in your own worth and abilities;
- motivation: the drive to succeed, to do your job well;
- a sense of mission: a strong belief in the value of what you are doing;
- enjoyment: satisfaction and personal fulfilment from doing your job;
- desire to learn: the urge to find out things, improve, progress;
- industry: the ability and willingness to work hard, not necessarily for an immediate reward;
- charisma, leadership: the ability to get people to listen to you, to do what you want.

These all appear, incidentally, in the profiles of the three successful but different teachers described in the research by Clarke et al. referred to earlier. Some are certainly more important than others, and individuals possess them to varying degrees.

Specific qualities
What are the personal qualities that contribute to *t*, that would not necessarily apply to doctors, nurses, counsellors or managers, but are teacher-specific? Here are some suggestions. It is interesting that I have found it very difficult to encapsulate these in single abstract nouns as I did the previous list:

- I sense where the learner is at, what their problem is; I feel what they know and don't know;
- I know how to transform what I know about the language into a form that is accessible to my learners;
- I know how to design and administer activities and exercises that will foster learning;
- I know when learning is and is not happening by the way the learners behave, I don't need tests;
- I get my 'buzz' from when the students succeed, learn, progress.

Interim summary 2
There is such a thing as a 'born teacher', in the sense that there are some people who come to teaching with certain personality characteristics that make them particularly fitted for the teaching

profession. These *t*-characteristics are multiple, each individual will therefore vary in how many they have and to what degree they have them. Probably some are more essential than others.

Related questions

If we accept the above as a working hypothesis, a number of questions need to be asked.

Can teachers with a very high *t*-factor teach well without training? Without experience?
It has been claimed by at least one respected educationist that a teacher with the necessary qualities needs no training (Haberman, 1995). But some of the *t*-qualities (motivation, desire to learn, awareness of learning processes) actually make a teacher particularly able to benefit from good training courses (those that make use of the teacher's own experience and critical reflective faculties as well as providing input). And that therefore though some brilliant teachers can manage without training, their performance is likely to be enhanced by it.

With regard to experience, the answer is even more definite. Even a 'born teacher' with all the qualities mentioned will always benefit from experience. Quite apart from the important process of automatising essential routines, and developing clearer perceptions of classroom processes, experience is also the main source of overall professional learning and progress. In fact, I would say that 'born teachers' will not be able to exploit their qualities to the full without it. Quite how much they do benefit from their experience depends, of course, on the *desire to learn* item listed previously.

Paradoxically, some very gifted 'born teachers' actually learn less because so much comes naturally: they find they can produce the kind of teaching behaviours almost by instinct that most of us have to learn through reflection on experience: so the necessity to learn to do better is not so obvious. In one sense they are lucky; on the other hand, they may reach a ceiling and cease to progress, while other less naturally gifted teachers continue to advance, and eventually overtake them. Such teachers are also unlikely to make good trainers: because so much of what they do is intuitive, they may find it difficult or impossible to explain to others how it is done.

Are there born non-teachers?
In my opinion, the answer to the question *Are there born non-teachers?* is yes. And if the deficiencies are deep enough and the person does not have the ability or motivation to remedy them, they will fail as a teacher and probably drop out of the profession fairly fast. If they do not, they and their learners have a problem!

Can people acquire *t*-characteristics through training and experience?
Some aspects of personality are extremely stable and hard to change. It is very difficult, for example, for someone to change their basic value system or personal motives for action. However, it is easier to learn the language better, to learn how to explain or elicit, to learn, perhaps, how to get on with people better.

Assuming that the person is reasonably intelligent, I would say that the only characteristics which you cannot do without are the motivation, industry and desire to learn. Intuitions about where a learner is at, and how to shape material in order to make it available to them – these are, I think, learnable through a combination of experience and reflection.

What are the implications for selection of future teachers?
Ideally, it would be desirable to test for the more essential of the teacher characteristics before admitting candidates to teacher training courses. What is very clear when initial selection is taking place is that mere knowledge of the language is a totally inadequate criterion. We need to find out something about the person's values, motives, and ability to empathise and communicate. The problem is that the specific teaching qualities only become apparent when the person actually starts teaching. And no-one has yet invented a test that reliably reveals whether a person has the motivation, commitment, etc. that will enable them to continue to learn. Probably you only find out if a person is going to make it after they start teaching. So it makes sense to have some kind of probation period before accepting novice teachers on the final stages of training and accreditation.

What are the implications for the design of training courses?
First, these are necessary. Certainly for those teachers who have only limited *t*-characteristics and need to develop or enhance them; and also for those teachers who possess them to a high degree and will be enabled through training and experience to exploit them to the full.

As to their content, assuming that the trainee enters with some *t*-characteristics, our job as trainers is to develop these, not teach them as if they didn't exist. In other words we should see teacher preparation as development rather than training. This does not mean not teaching techniques or not giving useful tips or information about the language: these are precisely the things we do need to teach, because the trainees may not have known them before. But the more basic approaches and principles are developed on the basis of what the trainee already knows and feels.

Above all, we need to be aware that each incoming teacher has a different constellation of *t*-qualities, and therefore, like the individual learner, needs space to develop his or her own learning programme.

Summary

There are people who come to teaching with a certain built-in propensity or disposition that makes them take to teaching more readily than others. However, this propensity is composed of not one but a number of *t*-factors, some of which are common to practitioners of a number of professions, some of which are teaching-specific. If they are not naturally possessed, some of these *t*-factors are difficult, sometimes impossible, to learn. People who lack some or all of these qualities may never become good teachers, or only with the greatest difficulty.

The *t*-factors on their own are not enough, however. Experience and some form of teacher training and/or development are necessary, and in fact more significant: so a teacher with all the necessary initial qualities who does not learn does not reach the same level of expertise as one who is less initially talented but who develops. People who possess these qualities to a high degree, and then proceed to enhance them through experience and learning are those we call 'born teachers'. So 'born teachers' are not necessarily eventually good teachers. And good teachers may not have been outstanding 'born teachers' to start with. Natural talent is no substitute for experience and professional development. It does give you a head-start; but as in a marathon race, eventual success does not depend on where you started, but on how far and how fast you run.

References

Bereiter C & M Scardamalia (1993) *Surpassing Ourselves: An Inquiry into the Nature and Implications of Expertise* Chicago: Open Court. (Referred to in Sternberg R T & J A Horvath 1995 A prototype view of expert teaching) *Educational Researcher* 24.6, 9–17

Clarke M A, A Davis, L K Rhodes & E Baker (1997) The coherence of practice in effective teaching. In Kumaravadivelu B & S M Gass (Eds) *Beyond Method: New Perspectives in Second and Foreign Language Education* New York: Cambridge University Press

Ellis R (1994) *The Study of Second Language Acquisition* Oxford: Oxford University Press

Haberman, M (1995) *Star Teachers of Children in Poverty* West Lafayette, Indiana: Kappa Delta Pi

Peterson P L & M A Comeaux (1987) Teachers' schemata for classroom events: the mental scaffolding of teachers *Teaching and Teacher Education* 3.4, 319–31

Richards J C, B Li & A Tang (1995) A comparison of pedagogical reasoning skills in novice and experienced ESL teachers *RELC Journal* 26.2, 1–24

Richards J C (1997) Experienced and less experienced teachers' uses of lesson plans. Talk given at *TESOL '97*, Orlando, Florida

Shulman L S (1986) Those who understand: knowledge growth in teaching *Educational Researcher* 15.2, 4–14

Ur P (1996) Can teaching be taught? *BRAZ-TESOL Newsletter* 10.4, 8–11

2.2 Helping teachers to reflect: Activities in training for action research

Barbara Thornton and Wasyl Cajkler, *University of Leicester*

The usefulness of Action Research (AR) in teacher development projects is generally acknowledged. However, it is perhaps tempting to underestimate what is required in terms of both reflective ability and research-related skills if teachers are to benefit from AR initiatives. In this workshop, we presented a number of activities which were used by in-service trainers with Spanish and Italian state school teachers engaged in a teacher development project, funded by the European Community *Socrates/Lingua* programme.

Preparatory activities

Sentence completion and questioning activities designed to help teachers to start out on AR were completed and evaluated at the beginning of the session. Participants commented on the usefulness of the activities in helping teachers to identify areas of AR focus and subsequent professional development projects. Following these, a questionnaire was presented and discussed to show how it could be administered to teachers to tease out the values and beliefs behind their classroom practice.

The activities explored in the first half of the workshop were designed to raise awareness of the many sources of ideas which are helpful in establishing an area for investigation. Thus, they demonstrated that the focus of AR projects might arise from a number of sources including feelings of dissatisfaction with the present, personal interest or concern, observing students, discussions with colleagues.

Observing practice on video

Heightening teachers' awareness is the key to change in behaviour. This can start from both negative and positive perceptions of existing practice. Awareness-raising was achieved in our project in a variety of ways: through written reflections and critical analysis, through peer observations in the classroom, and through video viewing of their own and others' practice.

Workshop participants observed a video using a *NADA* (Negative Aspect Deficit Approach) or a *PANDA* worksheet (Positive Aspect Non-Deficit Approach) to guide their observation. *NADA* approaches ask what the problem is and what can be improved; *PANDA* approaches look at the strengths and how these can be exploited for further development.

A lively exchange of views demonstrated the tension in AR projects. Taking a *NADA* view, the teacher observed on video had a strong pull to her right side, leading her to ignore students in part of the classroom. She also presented some examples of language in a decontextualised, 'non-authentic' way. *PANDA* responses, on the other hand, focused on the excellent rapport she had with pupils, the clarity of her explanation, and the response of the learners to her promptings.

Features of the activities

The activities evaluated in the workshop attempted to demonstrate that AR projects should:

- move away from the deficit model of AR towards a more exploratory non-judgemental approach
- be grounded in the realities of what actually takes place in classrooms
- take account of teachers' and students' personal theories of learning.

Engaging in the type of activity explored in this workshop, teachers were also given practice in other useful AR related skills: for example, data-gathering techniques, using observation instruments, peer feedback and teamwork.

2.3 Critical incidents: A comparison of Spanish and Israeli teachers

Peter James, *Universidad de Cantabria* **and Kari Smith,** *Oranim School of Education, Israel*

The Critical Incident (CI) is one of many tools used to develop reflectivity in teachers. The term 'critical incident' refers to an event or situation which marked a significant turning point in the life of a person. The vast majority of CIs are not dramatic or obvious, they are mostly accounts of commonplace events that occur in professional practice. These incidents appear to be typical rather than critical at first sight, but are rendered critical through analysis (Tripp D *Critical Incidents in Teaching: Developing Professional Judgement* 1993). CIs help teachers organise, clarify, and see connections between knowledge and personal theories by challenging their assumptions about education.

Recalling CIs is a means to help teachers focus their reflections. Kolb's model of experiential learning is the classic model of the reflective circle. (Kolb D A *Experiential Learning: Experience as the Source for Learning and Development* Prentice-Hall 1984) In this model, reflection is based on an experience which has taken place, and by reflecting on this experience, the teacher reaches alternative ways to approach a similar incident in the future, leading to professional growth. We believe, however, that experiences cannot be decontextualised from their setting (school, people involved, etc.). Ur's adaption of Kolb's model seems, therefore, to be more suitable for our purposes as it takes influences from external variables into account. (Ur P *A Course in Foreign Language Teaching: Practice and Theory* CUP 1996).

The main purpose of reflection is to lead to change, to professional growth. VanManen (1977) discusses three levels of reflectivity: technical, affective and political. The technical level deals with didactic skills, the affective level answers the question *How did my actions affect the pupils?* (empathy). The third level deals with the political and moral consequences of the teacher's actions. We have chosen to call this the evaluative level, relating it to moral and educational values of the teacher. Professional growth includes all three levels of reflection.

Methodology

Spanish and Israeli teachers were asked to write about CIs in their teaching career relating to the following questions: *What happened? Who was involved? What/Who made it happen? What did it feel like? For whom? What does it mean? To whom? Why did it happen? Did I like it? Was it a good thing? Why? What is it an example of? Whose classification? What do I do as a result of the CI?/ Should do? How? When? Where?* (adapted from Tripp, 1993).

Findings

It was found that CIs are a useful tool for helping teachers open up in spite of different cultures and different subjects taught. Most CIs reported were negative. In Israel the majority of CIs reported were related to pupils, while in Spain they were more related to language learning or teaching problems. It was found in both settings that teachers reflected at all three levels, technical, affective, and evaluative. The teachers' reaction to CIs as a tool for teacher education was positive in both settings.

Recommendations

CIs are most likely to work well in teacher education if the environment is supportive and the teachers are guided in their narration of CIs. They need to be pushed to various levels of reflection and learn to acknowledge the importance of learning from failure as well as from success.

2.4 Negotiating the social identity of the non-native EAL teacher

Anoma Siriwardena, *University of Nottingham*

The processes involved in teaching or learning English or any other language are not neutral, and inevitably influence and impact upon the social identities of teachers and learners. Some things may be gained, some may be lost, and many aspects of 'self' will be challenged and contested, as the norms of language use, values, beliefs and social and educational practices of one culture are placed alongside another.

Jim Cummins (1996) considers how ESL learners might 'negotiate' their identities for educational empowerment. I consider how non-native teachers of English as an Additional Language (EAL) might also empower themselves by negotiating 'their' social identities and better accessing their skills, experiences and knowledge as EAL learners and teachers and as users of other languages and other Englishes in their local environments.

EAL teacher identity

In EAL contexts where there are ambivalent attitudes towards the value of English and where the underlying sources for English language teaching methodology, materials, models of English, evaluation measures and educational practices derive largely from an Anglo-American perspective, the job of the non-native EAL teacher can be very constricted and cause conflicts. Conforming, consciously or unconsciously, to this kind of subject-positioning of teachers, learners and views of English language learning, without accounting more for local factors and teacher/learner identities in such contexts, can ultimately mean that for both teachers and learners more of one's 'self' is 'lost' than 'gained'.

Exploring teacher identity

As knowers of different languages and as learners of English(es) (native and local varieties), non-native EAL teachers bring a range of assets, experiences, knowledge, skills and resources to the EAL teaching and learning context which are not fully recognised and drawn upon, including their knowledge of the local socio-cultural context.

By engaging in a critical process of consciousness-raising, teachers can explore and make explicit ways in which they perceive themselves, their roles, strengths and theories and perceptions of language learning and teaching. Through such activities, it is hoped that teachers may be able to:

- better negotiate their 'own' identities for greater personal and professional self-awareness;
- better negotiate the job of EAL teaching within their particular local context/s by including a critical awareness of the wider sociopolitical and cultural implications of their role/s, as well as a sense of autonomy in utilising different views of language learning and teaching;
- identify areas they wish to change or develop further or gather more information on and the varied sources they might draw upon to facilitate this;

- use their strengths and resources to help learners to negotiate their identities as learners of English(es) in ways that do not disadvantage them.

In this way, the non-native EAL teacher's roles need not be conformist, constrictive and conflicting, but can become more critical, constructive and challenging.

2.5 How ELT professionals can help other members of staff

Andy Gillett, *University of Hertfordshire*

In my present job, I am often asked if I can help other members of staff, both academic and non-academic to communicate with international students better. The purpose of this presentation was to explore ways in which this might be done – how can intercultural communication be improved? How can we communicate better with a student from another culture, from another education system, of a different age, who speaks a different language?

I suggested that in order to communicate well with someone from a different culture, knowledge of that person's culture was necessary. This might be fine for people going to live in another country or for people who deal mainly with people from one or two other countries or cultures. However, this is impossible in a large university which could have students from 80 different countries. I felt the most important objective of any training course was to raise people's awareness of areas of difference. I said that I had found it useful to look at five broad areas:

Cultural behaviour

People from different cultures do things in different ways. We need to increase our awareness of and sensitivity to culturally different modes of behaviour. We need to recognise different cultural patterns at work in the behaviour of people from other countries and cultures. We need to be aware of how our own cultural background influences our behaviour. And we need to develop tolerance for behaviour patterns that are different from our own. Tomalin and Stempleski (*Cultural Awareness* OUP 1993) have some useful exercises.

Students' perception/expectations of learning

How do students see the learning process? What is the role of the tutor? What part is the student expected to play in all this? What are the conventions in British HE? What can students expect and what is expected of them? Clear procedures are necessary. Jin and Cortazzi (In Graddol, Thompson and Byram (Eds.) *Language and Culture* Multilingual Matters 1993) is a useful starting point for discussion.

Culture

Culture is an inherited wealth in which we all can share, but it is passed on to us from different sources, and we share it in different parts with different groups to which we belong. What cultures do lecturers and international students share? What knowledge is expected/presupposed? Bowers (*ELTJ* 46 1992) is useful here.

Cross cultural pragmatics

Understanding what is meant by what is said. Thomas (*Meaning in Interaction* Longman 1995) has some useful ideas. Tannen (*That's Not What I Meant* Virago 1992) has some good examples.

Advice for teaching

Lectures: clear organisation – signalling; support with writing, visuals, handouts; take care over handwriting; provide reading before lecture.

Speaking: don't keep changing subject; signpost; summarise often; repeat if necessary; be careful of background knowledge assumed; avoid unfamiliar, idiomatic or technical English – use formal language; be careful of speed of delivery, clear pauses, etc.; pronounce clearly; do not talk while eating or with back to audience; be careful of background noise, etc.; organise questions; be explicit.

Assignments: clear instructions for coursework; provide clear feedback on written work; set written coursework early in order to identify problems; set exams as late in the course as possible.

General: provide simplified brochure/application form; provide international student tutor; don't try and answer grammar questions – give a model of good English; leave grammatical explanations to the experts; assume different expectations.

2.6 Designer teaching

Scott Thornbury, *International House, Barcelona*

What help is on offer for teachers – especially new ones – who lose sleep over lesson planning? The kind of advice traditionally given consists of offering either lesson planning maxims ('lessons should be varied and flexible ...') and/or lesson macro-structures or templates such as the much maligned PPP format.

The advantage for the novice teacher of having a template on which to map planning decisions is that this provides a schema, or script, for the lesson, and thus would seem to replicate the kind of planning strategies of experienced teachers. The debate over the relative merits of the PPP script compared with other, e.g. fluency-driven, ones is probably rather academic.

For a start, in the vast majority of ELT contexts, teachers are working within the *Type A* paradigm: that is, they are working from syllabuses of pre-selected, discrete linguistic items, a curricular choice that precludes anything but a presentation methodology, whether we like it or not. Moreover, from the point of view of the learners, their expectations regarding lesson structure are probably influenced less by abstract pedagogical models than by the concrete experience of other lessons, and (this is my point) of other performance genres, such as film and music.

A student survey I conducted which investigated metaphors for the classroom experience suggested that lessons can be characterised in aesthetic terms. Good lessons have *plot*, as opposed to *story* (in E M Forster's formulation). That is, their stages are linked logically (as opposed to simply sequentially), and they embed a complication that, in turn, requires a resolution. In other words, good lessons problematise the learning experience.

Lessons also have rhythm. As Doyle says, 'Time does not simply pass in classrooms. Rather, there is rhythmic movement toward the accomplishment of academic and socio-interactional ends'. (In Wittrock M C (Ed.) 1986 (3rd edition) *Handbook of Research on Teaching* New York: MacMillan.) And they have flow: it is the lack of fluidly automated routines that characterises the stop-start nature of novices' lessons. Good lessons also have a coherent and unitary theme, that is, the answer to the question 'What was the lesson about?'

Finally, good lessons have, in Kermode's term, 'a sense of an ending'. This expectation of closure (as opposed to drift) serves to structure the learning experience and make it purposeful, but without imposing on it the techno-rational 'achievement of aims' scenario so beloved by examining bodies. (I would argue that good lesson design originates less in the formulation of explicit aims than in a more generalised notion of 'fit'.)

What are the implications from a training and development perspective?

Provide trainee teachers with a menu of lesson templates and provide opportunities to become fluent in a limited range of routines. Invite trainees to observe lessons aesthetically, applying notions of plot, rhythm, flow, theme, and ending. 'Take pains. Be perfect. Adieu.'

2.7 Can colleges produce reflective teachers?

Radka Perclova, *Association of Teachers of English in the Czech Republic*

The aim of our project was to support undergraduate teacher trainees in making links between TEFL theory and practice, to provide them with opportunities for experiential learning, to facilitate their reflection, to encourage their responsibility for their own learning, and to respect their individual styles. To achieve the objectives, the trainees were led to make several gradual steps:

- they devised their own assessment criteria for peer-teaching and peer-presentations and steadily enriched them;
- they were provided with tasks on observation sheets for their observation of mentors;
- reflection on the tasks was fostered in seminars;
- they produced observation sheets for classes taught by their peers during a one-block teaching practice conducted under the guidance of their mentor;
- they wrote self-evaluations of the teaching practice to which the trainer responded;
- amendments to the syllabus were made accordingly.

The steps connected with the teaching practice were repeated during the second and the third one-block practices. Brief background reading on different areas of observation focus was discussed with trainees and distributed to them before the second practice.

The materials trainees produced were evaluated. While several trainees just copied tasks from observation sheets they had been given, others came up with innovative ideas which they evolved continuously. The best results were achieved when trainees drew attention to one simple issue, e.g. their peers' responses to pupils' effort, giving instructions, the frequency of pupils' contributions, and dealing with errors. Success also heavily depended on the quality of peer collaboration. When examining the trainees' reflections and the development of these systems, trainees' reflection on the lessons and the evaluation of the teaching practice were utilised. Some trainees' schemata were challenged, as were their attitudes to learners and instruction giving.

A questionnaire was prepared to enable a view of the project from different perspectives. The EFL teacher training methodology course was separated into 27 individual components. Trainees assessed how important the specific components were for equipping them with the qualities of a competent teacher. The components the trainees considered extremely important read as follows: teaching classes during their teaching practice, preparation of lessons during teaching practice, presentation of practical techniques by the tutor, and mentors' feedback on their lessons. In an additional part of the questionnaire, the trainees were asked about the change in their opinions on teaching. The majority of them strongly agreed that their constructs had changed and they also strongly agreed that this change was connected with their methods of teaching.

Surprisingly, trainees considered theoretical input very important (maybe influenced by the Czech academic tradition), though at the same time it was again practice that worked wonders, according to them. Reflection seemingly became part of their repertoire, as could be seen from the high marks given to the importance of the preparation of their lessons.

2.8 A process approach to language awareness in Cambridge RSA/CELTA courses

Heather Westrup, *Freelance*

According to Philip Kerr (1993), on 70% of CELTA courses the language awareness component is conducted through a knowledge transfer mode in which the content is exclusively an examination of the verb phrase with only a cursory link to the methodology strand of the course.

Drawing on my experience as a primary teacher, the memory of my needs as a new EFL teacher and as a trainer in other contexts, as well as being encouraged by an emerging discontent with present practice as reported in the literature, I decided to introduce a process approach to the LA component. This was intended to be enabling rather than knowledge based. The content and procedures were closely integrated with other areas of the syllabus. The clearly defined topic areas of the 1996 CELTA syllabus made this cross-curricular design more apparent.

With this syllabus and my own experience in mind, I saw the broad aims for the LA component as:

1 To allay fears about learning and teaching grammar.
2 To instil in trainees a fascination with language and a desire to continue the investigations into language begun on this course.
3 To give trainees the tools with which to cope with language in the classroom, satisfy (2) and, as a consequence, satisfy (1).

Scheme of work

1 Introduction – the basics and some terminology (1,4,6)
2 Researching and recording language items (1,6)
3 Context, appropriacy and the functional approach (1,2,3,4,5)
4 Language and the learner (1,2,4)
5 Language and the coursebook (1,3,4,5)
6 Language and the lesson/scheme of work (1,3,4,5)
7 Word order and practical syntax (1,4,5,6)
8 Introduction to discourse (1,4)
9 Workshop to prepare trainees' individual Language Projects (1,2,3,4,5,6)
10 Presentations of trainees' Language Projects (poster presentation) (1,2,3,4,5,6)

Figures in brackets refer to 1996 Syllabus topic areas addressed during this session.

The first three sessions aimed at giving trainees the confidence, motivation and basic tools to study language in a broad sense. Sessions 4 to 6 linked this with an introduction to language acquisition, language comparisons and language teaching methods and materials. Sessions 7 and 8 were particularly necessary for trainees going to teach in tertiary institutions. Sessions 9 and 10 pulled all the threads together and provided informal assessment. The materials used were all authentic or student generated and the procedures included modelling, discussion, project work, loop input and other techniques drawn from contemporary language teaching methodology.

The scheme appeared to satisfy the aims and objectives well and when considered in the light of the 1996 CELTA Syllabus was seen as a model of good teaching and therefore good training practice. There was a marked effect on the motivation and ability of trainees to do research for their teaching, to understand their students' problems, and to reflect intelligently on materials and teaching methodology. They were provided with a strong initial impetus to continue practising professional development after the course.

Contact address: *48 Oxford Road, Cambridge CB4 3PW, UK*

2.9 How effective is a task-based methodology in teacher education?

Simon Etherton, *University of Exeter*

Drawing on findings from an ongoing small-scale inquiry, this paper addresses the reality of learning through task-based interaction in teacher education and explores some strategies for making the use of tasks in teacher education more effective.

The rationale for using tasks

The use of tasks in teacher education is based on a number of important principles of learning:

- learning is a process of actively constructing knowledge and developing conceptual frameworks;
- learning is knowledge dependent: the known should inform and be informed by the new. This is described by Piaget's twin concepts of *assimilation* (changing the new to fit with the known) and *accommodation* (modifying the known to take account of the new);
- learning is connected to the situation and the context of the student teachers and the training programme;
- learning is a social process enhanced by interaction with others.

Tasks require student teachers to reflect on their individual experiences, knowledge and beliefs, to interact with each other, and to share these personal theories. The task input and activities enable new knowledge to be collaboratively explored and constructed, but with each individual developing their own personally significant outcomes.

The reality of task-based learning – some findings

Questionnaires revealed that student teachers were very positive about the benefits of working in groups on a task. Regardless of task type and content, they all found the process of sharing ideas the most informative and enjoyable aspect of undertaking tasks. Despite this enthusiasm, transcripts of group interaction often showed uneven participation, both in quantity and quality. They also showed that groups would be influenced by initial comments and suggestions, and many issues would not be addressed. The discussion was frequently superficial and anecdotal with issues not being explored in any real depth. Contributions were rarely questioned or challenged and the talk was often cumulative.

Implications for practice

If student teachers are to learn effectively from tasks, they need to become aware of a number of communication and cooperative skills and strategies.

Firstly, exploratory talk (Mercer N 1995 *The Guided Construction of Knowledge* Clevedon: Multilingual Matters) should be encouraged. Student teachers should learn to engage critically, but constructively, in each other's ideas. Exploratory talk can be developed by analysing talk from transcripts and videos. The question *What makes talk effective?* should be addressed.

Secondly, student teachers need to discuss and recognise how to make group work more effective. The importance of roles within groups, such as clarifying, summarising and supporting, should be addressed and experienced, possibly in a cooperative language learning loop. Issues of developing group dynamics could also be learnt this way.

Thirdly, tasks should have an element of individual reflection before interaction takes place. This raises awareness of personal ideas and results in a more rounded discussion with more balanced participation, and also enables change and development to become more visible.

Conclusions

Tasks should effectively enable student teachers to develop their knowledge and understanding of teaching. However, I believe that it is only by explicitly developing skills of interaction and cooperation that the quality of talk, thought and learning can be enhanced.

2.10 They neither prosper nor perish – the EFL profession reviewed

Trevor Doble, *Nelson English School*

'Teachers are ... at the bottom of the professional heap ... And I wasn't even a real teacher. The only remarkable thing about me was the fact that I was still doing a holiday job at the age of forty. I was ... another over-educated, under motivated loser who had missed his chance and drifted into the Sargasso Sea of EFL work.' (Dibden M *Dirty Tricks* 1991)

One would hope that things have improved since the above was written. Certainly my interviews with EFL teachers for my MEd dissertation seemed to reinforce rather than reject the above sentiments.

There are four areas that point towards EFL being regarded as a non-profession:

Commitment
My research noted a distinct lack of initial commitment by the teachers – there was a general drift into EFL teaching after trying other occupations, with travel given as the main reason for entering EFL. Professions require a strong commitment from the outset.

Adequate body of knowledge
Any profession has a body of knowledge that takes many years to acquire and use. The EFL industry accepts graduates and non-graduates, producing inevitable variations in quality. In addition, one must ask if a four-week preparatory course is sufficient in terms of a knowledge base.

Autonomy

Most professionals are autonomous and able to act independently. Teachers, however, seem to be just salaried workers, and EFL teaching long ago sold its soul to the business ethic, so that teachers are left alone as long as their classes are profitable, but are called to account the moment losses are made.

Status and prestige

Teachers have suffered from a bad press, with EFL teaching viewed in many countries as one step up the ladder from grape picking. At the moment, many teachers seem to be facing a career crunch, having realised that TEFL has led them into a vocational cul-de-sac.

2.11 'Shorts'

Self-awareness as a core component of a culture course curriculum, *Inge Brown, Freelance and Anne-Marie Tanahashi, Washington State Community College Consortium for Kobe*

The idea of perceptual difference is one of the simplest and yet one of the most challenging ideas to internalise. It is the idea that everyone perceives the world differently but that members of one culture group share basic sets of perceptions which differ from those sets of perceptions shared by other culture groups. As David Hoppes says 'It is not that the idea is difficult to understand, it is that it is hard to impose upon ourselves, to internalise so that if affects our behaviour' (in Pusch M D, 1979).

In our culture courses, we should be helping our students to become flexible in their perceptions and not to constantly view things through the same cultural lens. This will help students to see more clearly, which is the first step towards cultural awareness.

Issues in initial teacher training, *Jenny Pugsley, Trinity College London*

The individual's reactions to change depend partly on the sector(s) with which they identify: research, academic/teaching, teacher training, assessment of teacher training (examination and validation bodies), direct language teaching, trained or in-training or would-be teacher, professional body or trade association, funding council or national funding body, publishing.

Training the trainers: A process approach in action, *Keith Morrow, Freelance, and Wilfried van Rompaey, Katholieke Hogeschool Limburg, Belgium*

The philosophy of the course was summarised as follows:

- teacher training is a person-centred activity, not a set of pre-determined formulae

- dare to share
- the content of the course is the process.

Wilfried showed an extract from his course journal which dated back to the first days of the course and showed his initial scepticism. Yet eventually he realised that any training programme revolves around the concept of change. Change for him related to the positive impact of personal relationships within the international context, an increased openness to learning-by-doing and to groupwork, and to his participation in several participant-led sessions.

Trainer training in Central Slovakia – is personal development the answer? *Phil Dexter, The British Council Slovakia, and Nora Tomkova, Metodické Centrum, Banska Bystrica, Slovakia*

Participants considered that in planning presentations it is important to consider both psychological preparation as well as content. Such issues as getting into a positive mood, being ready to face the challenge and thorough preparation were considered to be important. Feedback could concentrate on the presentation style, the materials, the topic. It was considered that this kind of focused feedback was more relevant than general comments.

The trainer-trainee relationship: La vie en rose? *Gabriela S Matei, University of Timisoara*

In an inquiry-oriented approach to initial teacher education, both teacher educator and trainees are teaching, learning and researching. As teacher educator, I have been teaching, but also learning a lot from my trainees: they have been teaching me their experience as student teachers and their experience as researchers on teaching and learning. At the same time, we are all researching: schools, teachers, pupils, educational processes, each other, ourselves, etc. The borders between teaching, learning and researching have become so blurred as to disappear completely in many situations in which we have interacted.

This process places new demands on the trainees, who have to assume almost full responsibility for their professional development as teacher-researchers, while providing information about their experiences to the trainer-researcher.

Teaching Japanese students – what to expect, *Joyce Roth, Seian Girls' High School, Kyoto*

In the beginning of the Japanese school year as I begin my secondary courses in reading, writing, and oral work, my time is taken up more by arranging than teaching. I give my girls lessons on what I expect of them and painstakingly shape the behavior I want. In the long run, it pays off with these Japanese learners actively participating in the lessons, and, for many, success when and if they study abroad. For those of you who haven't gotten already trained students, don't expect your Japanese learners to figure out how to 'do it'. Take the time to show them and teach them, and then enjoy their contribution to your classes.

Mentor training: Which way to go? *Tamas Kiss, Bessenyei Gyorgy Teacher Training College, Hungary*

In a recent survey on mentor training, mentors and university tutors were asked about the possible future directions for mentor training. As a result the following list was compiled:

- pre-lesson help (discussion, lesson planning, etc.)
- observation skills
- providing post-lesson feedback
- assessment
- counselling skills (of course not a whole programme but sub-skills like *listening to others*)
- methodology up-date which is not more than 30% of the programme
- professional issues like roles, models of mentoring, etc.

Revitalising your teaching, *Katie Head, Eurocentre Cambridge and Pauline Taylor, Christchurch College of Education, New Zealand*

Working with activities from our book *Readings in Teacher Development* (Heinemann 1997), we introduced participants attending the workshop to a number of strategies for developing this awareness and working on areas of potential change in their own teaching. Some activities were done in pairs or groups, while others involved silent, private reflection. They are briefly summarised below:

- Tell a partner what you like about your own teaching. Feeling good about what you do already is an important basis for exploring change. Change happens most easily when people are in a positive frame of mind.
- List some areas of your own teaching that you would like to be better at. After a period of private reflection, participants chose one of the areas they had listed, and explained it to a partner. Talking through a topic with a good listener often helps to clarify and focus it.
- Identify ten beliefs that you have about good teaching. We provided our own list as an example, and asked people to identify and write down some personal beliefs. Consider how far your teaching reflects these beliefs and values. Notice the areas where what you actually do is different from what you believe you should do. Using a metaphor borrowed from Chris Aldred, we described as 'worms' the negative messages that eat away at our good intentions. These might be negative student responses, or our own inner doubts about what may happen in practice. Participants were asked to write some 'worms' beside each of their beliefs, and notice the gaps between belief and practice. These are potential development areas.
- (In groups) Brainstorm all the little 'rules' that operate in your teaching, and consider the worst that might happen if you actually decided to change any of them. This more light-hearted activity, based on Fanselow's *Breaking Rules* approach, encouraged participants to own up to some of their more ridiculous classroom habits, and reconsider their usefulness.

Integration of EFL within university academic subject specialty content curriculum, *Alan Brady and Michael Lynn, Kwansei Gakuin University*

In recent years private Japanese universities have employed teams of western foreign language faculty, both tenured and contracted, to co-lead the development and implementation of campus EFL curricular innovations and programs. Although this strategy has helped create a progressive international image for some universities and open up the job market to more instructors with graduate degrees in TESL/TEFL, at the same time it has had an anaesthetising effect on the Japanese academic community by removing them from responsible involvement in the process of improving EFL curricula. As a result, not only has the opportunity for truly internationalising the process through on-going intercultural negotiation between Japanese and Western academic faculty been minimised, but in some cases these new programs have ironically weakened the status of EFL teaching by segregating it from the specific purposes it could serve in non-language departments.

3 MATERIALS: NEW IDEAS, NEW PRACTICE

3.1 Writing readers

Philip Prowse, *Freelance*

Before starting

As a teacher decide on your level and think of a class you know or have recently taught at that level. Use them as your reference point, not just for language, but also for content. Later, if you are lucky, you may be able to try the material out with the actual class, or a similar one.

Getting started

It is recognised that much good modern fiction defies genre, creating its own contexts and values. However, the learner of English as a reader is helped by as many reference points as possible. There is a conflict here between the potentially good story which defies genre, and one within a genre. Using genre, a successful way to start is to move like this:

Genre → Character → Situation → Place → Event.

In other words, think of a genre which readers will be familiar with either through reading or through TV and video. Examples include Adventure, Detective, Thriller, Romance, Disaster, Travel, Fantasy, Science Fiction, Historical, Horror.

How to proceed

Think of a character, the kind that appears in your chosen genre. Place the character in a situation, some kind of problem or opportunity. Choose the place, the physical location. Then think of an event that the character participates in. And let the story begin ...

This way of writing is for those who want to find out what happens to the character and who write the story in order to do so. The advantage of this 'making it up as you go along' method is that you can, of course, go back and plant plot trails and introduce clues and characters when the need arises.

Cultural setting

The cultural setting of the story is paramount. The readers do not have to have direct personal experience of the setting but must know what to expect. Thus a western/cowboy story will draw on a lot of background knowledge from TV and film westerns, while a story set in Africa in the First World War will be much more demanding and therefore difficult. The setting does not need to be in Britain or the USA or an English-speaking country as long as the readers are aware of the cultural givens, or they are explained as part of the story (e.g. the problems a westerner living in Tibet would face).

Pastiche can be very successful. Consider taking a modern classic and writing a sequel.

The look on the page

Processing large chunks of text is more difficult in a new language than short paragraphs. Use dialogue as much as possible.

Tips from Raymond Chandler and other great non-writers of readers!

- Always leave a chapter or page unfinished so that when you start again you are right in the thick of it and not staring at a blank page.
- 1,000 words a day is a good aim.
- 'If in doubt, have a man with a gun come in the door...' (or some other dramatic event).

Correspondence address: *27 Owlstone Rd, Cambridge CB3 9JH, UK*

3.2 How good are graded readers?

David R Hill, *University of Edinburgh*

Graded Readers enable students to practise English outside the classroom, develop a competence in reading extended text and provide a stimulus for writing, speaking and listening. No other resource is so varied in content or level and many titles are excellent. I believe, however, that improvements could be made in six areas:

Size of font
There is a tendency to use fonts that are too small and too faint. This may save on paper and ink but makes reading much harder for students who have little experience of reading and whose mother tongue is written in a different script.

Simplifications
Many titles, especially film tie-ins, are blow-by-blow accounts that read like précis. Successful simplifications present a selection of scenes in depth and at length, allowing the learners to draw breath and absorb the setting and characters.

Simple originals
Simple originals at intermediate level and above tend to lack interest. Editors need to recruit authors who create interesting characters and have a message to put across.

Transition to unsimplified books
There is a need for longer books at the upper levels. At the moment very few graded readers go beyond 120 pages, while very few L1 best sellers are shorter than 300 pages. These longer books might begin with graded language and end with the original text.

Non-fiction
To be at all interesting, factual subjects need to be well researched and written at least at an intermediate level. The most promising way forward would be to produce an EFL edition of non-fiction titles published by Usborne and Dorling-Kindersley.

Aids to reading
At the moment most series offer an introduction and a glossary that help the learner, and a set of exercises that help the teacher. Indeed the current trend is for publishers to offer more and more aids for teaching. These neither help the learner nor encourage good methodology among teachers.

Study editions of the most popular titles could contain:

- an introduction that prepares the student not only for understanding and appreciating the content of the book but also for the new lexis and syntax;
- two or three review sections in the course of the book that would confirm the students' understanding of the story so far and lead them into the next section;
- a final section inviting students to reflect on what they have read and pointing them to other titles with a similar theme or setting.

Plain text versions would be available for those who did not want any distraction. *Study editions* would help the very large number of students (and teachers) who are not good at reading fiction, and they would make it clear to educators, parents and students that reading graded readers was serious and useful as well as enjoyable.

3.3 Taiwan students discover the British murder mystery

Johanna E Katchen, *National Tsing Hua University, Taiwan*

As cable television becomes more widespread in East Asia, we can view more English programmes from abroad. Yet even though English has been a required subject in the schools for a number of years, the level of most secondary school graduates is not nearly high enough to comprehend English films or television shows without assistance. Cable television companies are, therefore, providing English programmes with L1 subtitles to get a wider market. Thus it is no longer practical to ignore this source of spoken English.

Fourteen students on a university advanced listening class were each given a copy of an episode from either *Inspector Morse* or *The Ruth Rendell Mysteries* spoken in the original British English varieties and subtitled in Chinese. All the students had been judged on the basis of previous courses as having high intermediate to advanced levels of English. The students had five to six weeks to complete the project. They had to summarise the story, transcribe a five-minute portion of the video, comment on the helpfulness or distraction of the subtitles (citing specific examples), and comment on their own listening ability with regard to the programme.

The results seem to indicate that most technical and semi-technical vocabulary can be accessed and learned through L1 subtitles. Students reported learning, for example, *excommunication*, *infirmary*,

Goths. Thus it may be that programmes on specific topic areas that do not require specialised knowledge (documentaries and other information programmes) would be most useful for acquiring new English vocabulary through L1 subtitles by means of self-study. Idioms, slang and culture-specific references were more difficult for students to comprehend, though students with higher levels of listening were able to access more; some reported learning, for example, *cock-and-bull story* and *I don't buy it*. This may mean that popular genres such as the situation comedy would produce better learning, especially at lower levels, with a classroom teacher and/or English captions.

While students complained about British English (American is the variety taught in Taiwan), they nevertheless reported learning pronunciation differences (as in *can't*) and becoming more sensitive to British varieties; Chinese subtitles were of great help here. Better listeners said Chinese subtitles were too distracting for ordinary viewing, when getting the main ideas was enough. For learning to listen to new or uncommon vocabulary though, all acknowledged the potential usefulness of L1 subtitles. The best students enjoyed comparing the English and Chinese; in some cases, they found mistakes or omissions and even suggested better Chinese translations. Other students commented that the L1 subtitles helped them to guess, and this was important for this type of programme, where information is conveyed mostly through speech rather than through action and there are one or more subplots. Most importantly, all students reported learning something about their listening skills, learning strategies, or vocabulary from this assignment.

3.4 A story journey

Andrew Wright

Seventy people set off on a story journey. This is how it was organised:

Before the participants came into the room

1) Seventy chairs in pairs, back to back, scattered about the room.

2) On each chair a variety of objects and pictures: postcards, leaves and stones, a sweet, etc.

Before the journey

1) Pairs. Each pair given a picture of a fool derived from Tarot designs. Each pair studies their fool and decides what he or she might be: *name*, *job*, etc.

2) Each pair decides on the genre of their story journey: *love*, *horror*, *crime*, etc.

3) The whole group brainstorm words for feelings. Individuals choose several of them. Pairs then choose three and put them into the order they want them to occur in their story. For example, *sad*, *angry*, *happy*.

4) Introduction to the chairs: each chair is a village. Your fool can stay in one village or travel from village to village. The objects and pictures are what happens to your fool. Pick up the objects and pictures to look at them but replace them.

The journey

1) Pairs take their fool through his or her journey (inventing his or her story based on the pictures and objects on the chairs and guided by the decisions about the story genre and the list of feelings).

2) After about ten minutes the 'story travellers' stop and pass the evening (about five minutes) telling their story to a neighbouring pair of story travellers.

3) Each pair then tries to incorporate something from the other pair's story into their own story.

4) When all three feelings have been incorporated into the story and the story is finished the pairs make sure they can remember their story.

Storytelling after the journey

1) New pairs: each story traveller takes his or her new partner through their fool's story, actually re-tracing his or her steps from chair to chair.

Discussion

Groups discussed what adaptations would have to be made for two different fluency levels. Proposals were made to make the organisation a little simpler (for example, a single route) and also for how to give linguistic support (for example, helpful words and phrases on each chair). It was also suggested that the story travellers might be allowed to pick up the objects or pictures and to lay them out on a table, in sequence, when their story is ready.

(This session was based on the book *Creating Stories with Children* OUP.)

3.5 Story-sharing evening

Andrew Wright

What a lovely variety of stories this year! There were family stories, personal anecdotes and traditional stories. Some people came intending to tell a story and didn't and other people came to sit quietly and listen and found themselves telling a story. At the end of the evening, one participant said how happy he had been to discover two stories within himself! So the evening flowed by very nicely.

By the way, how good it was to hear an African story! That lovely combination of telling and singing! If only we could have more stories from our African colleagues and, indeed, from a much wider range of cultures represented by the **IATEFL** membership.

Proposal: A book of IATEFL stories!

What about an **IATEFL** book of short stories for the newly conceived **IATEFL** list of publications! If you might be willing to contribute a story, then please use these guidelines:

1) Any type of story: personal, myth, legend, fable or fiction. If the story is copyright then you must tell us.

2) Short: no more than about 800 words, preferably less. If the story is longer, then it must be divided into sections which have a dramatic unity to them.

3) Some suggestions for how the story might be used in class (activities) and with whom (level).

4) Please submit the story on disc in ASCII, Word for Windows or WordPerfect together

with hard copy. Hardcopy without disk will be accepted but makes more work for me. A handwritten story will be considered but it makes much more work for me! Don't worry about the accuracy of the English – it can be modified to conform.

5) In order to minimise the work for me, please accept that I must have the editor's right to use or to reject a story. Also accept that the book will only be published if there are enough appropriate contributions.

6) If a story is accepted, then the contributor's name will be given with the story.

7) If a story is modified, the contributor will be consulted.

8) Any profits from the book will go to **IATEFL** – no royalty or fee to the contributors or editor.

Send your contributions to: *Andrew Wright, Korosfoi utca 2, Godollo, 2100 Hungary.*

3.6 Visual support and vocabulary learning

Agnieszka Lenko-Szymanska,
University of Łódź

In my talk I tried to answer the questions *What makes a picture an effective teaching aid?* and *Are some visuals better than others?*

Visuals have their communicative validity. Even though language seems to be the most universal code of communication, humans do not give up communicating through pictures. Examples from everyday life include traffic signs and the *Windows* computer environment. The reason for the use of the visual code as an alternative code of communication is the fact that certain information, such as shape, size, colour and the structure of physical objects as well as various relations among objects and abstract concepts, is expressed better by pictures than words.

Visuals also have their psychological validity. In addition to being one of the codes for conveying information, pictures, along with words, are one of the two internal codes of cognitive processes. In other words, we think not only in words but also in pictures.

Visuals have a considerable mnemonic value: they are remembered better than words. They also have a great affective value; they easily evoke feelings and attitudes which strengthen retention. Additionally, using pictures in vocabulary training influences the organisation of the mental lexicon. Thanks to visuals, beginners more quickly develop the compound structure of the mental lexicon in which L2 words are connected directly with the related concepts without the mediation of L1. This type of organisation increases learners' proficiency. Visual support also has a great organisational value and arranged information is remembered better. Visual presentation of verbal material (for example in a form of a wordtree) helps to retain it better in a well-structured form. Moreover, visuals increase cultural awareness, easily depicting the differences between such culture-loaded words as *sink*, *tap* or *house*.

In my talk I tried to prove that visuals have a much greater role to play than just to illustrate the meaning of concrete nouns and other easily depictable words. I showed that they can also illustrate abstract words such as *maternity*. Pictures can express metaphoric extensions of some words, for example ***enter*** *the market*, or just show the logical relations among vocabulary items through the use of diagrams such as wordtrees.

Finally, the factors influencing the effectiveness of visuals were discussed. They are visual distinctiveness (the more distinct the pictures the better), simplicity (simple pictures are more effective than complex ones depicting many items), degree of detail (young children prefer realistic pictures, adults prefer schematic ones), clarity and size (pictures have to be clear and easily visible to be effective).

3.7 Working with (un)limited resources

Charlie and Jill Hadfield

Our materials for teaching elementary and low intermediate students in low tech environments are being published by OUP later this year under the title *Keep it Simple*. For almost two decades, we have been alternating working in the developing world with work in the UK (relatively high tech) and are very concerned about the problems facing teachers of large classes in poorly resourced environments. Our materials try in a simple, practical way to show how much can be done in the way of real communicative, humanistic teaching, by focusing on the almost unlimited resources of the people in the classroom, rather than worrying unduly about a lack of physical resources.

In *Keep it Simple*, forty topics run across each of five areas (presentation, oral practice, listening, reading, writing) making a total of 200 separate activities, which can be used either separately as an addition to textbooks or other course material (i.e. as a type of teacher resource book) or by teachers to make a completely self-contained course of study. Our object is to provide teachers with practical, useful, complete material in a form which does not require each student to have access to a textbook. In many countries, textbook provision is an impossibility due to the expense involved, the lack of paper, or problems of distribution. In addition many textbook projects have resulted in methodologically or culturally unsuitable teaching materials being brought in. Our approach can be valuable in both high tech environments like the UK, as well as in less well favoured classrooms around the globe. Five main types of activity are used: pair work/information gap activities; outline and variation; student-produced materials; humanistic; visualisation.

A brief introduction to this thinking behind the materials, and an outline of the structure of the book, was followed by practical demonstrations of each of the five activity types. Concrete demonstrations of the use of cheap, universally available materials such as washing lines, clothes pegs, and large posters involved the sixty participants (a typical large class) in practical exercises, pairwork with different posters at either end of the room, with students sitting back to back, small group work discussions of a poster, visualisation of a landscape, and mass jigsaw reading.

Contact address: *Rivermead, Combeinteignhead, Newton Abbot, Devon TQ12 4RR, UK*

3.8 Authentic listening materials and strategic listening

John Field, *University of Cambridge*

The term authentic is generally taken to apply to any materials which have not been specially designed for a second language learner. This means that authentic listening materials cover a wide spectrum of styles from formal (an interview) and even 'read aloud' (the radio news) to very informal (a pub conversation). It is imprecise to treat authentic as synonymous with 'conversational'. Authentic materials stand in contra-distinction to scripted materials and to materials whose language has been graded to fit the knowledge of the learner.

Authentic listening passages exemplify the cadences of natural speech in a way that scripted materials do not – so it is desirable to introduce them at an early stage of learning. This implies that learners at lower levels may encounter authentic materials alongside scripted ones. A bridge between the two is necessary, with teachers introducing learners systematically to the features of conversational speech. The best way of achieving this is to play short pieces from authentic texts which exemplify hesitation markers, false starts, loosely coordinated syntax, etc., and to ask learners to transcribe what they hear.

Semi-authentic materials

Teachers do well to record their own authentic listening passages from the radio and TV. But teachers who use commercially produced materials or are preparing learners for international exams may find themselves working with what are termed 'semi-authentic passages'. These are of two types:

Improvised – actors role-playing a situation in a studio
Re-recorded – actors reproducing a real-life speech event from a transcript.

During this talk, listening texts of four types (scripted, improvised, re-recorded and authentic) were played, and participants had little difficulty in distinguishing them. A piece of research was then presented, in which an actress re-recorded an authentic piece of text from a radio programme (a recording of explorers confronted by bears). A number of differences were noted in the re-recorded version, including greater use of full-quality forms, greater pausing and more frequent, regular and logical sentence stress.

Re-recorded materials evidently differ considerably from authentic ones – and (importantly) the ways in which they differ mark word boundaries more clearly for the listener than is usual in natural speech.

Real-life listening

The use of authentic materials gives rise to a very different type of listening in the classroom from that which (on the basis of experience with scripted or graded materials) we tend to expect. Recognition of words in the text is usually far from complete, and listeners depend very much, as they do in real life, upon guessing links between the fragmented pieces which they understand. Evidence was presented that many of the words in an authentic narrative text were recognised by an average of only about 15–20% of a group of lower intermediate learners – though recognition rose to about 90% for particularly salient or frequent words. This supports a view of L2 listening as highly strategic. It was argued that we need to adapt the structure of our lessons to reflect the real-life process of isolating a few known words and then forming guesses based upon context. We need to show learners that guessing is not a mark of failure – to encourage the more timid ones to take risks and to show the bolder ones the importance of checking hypotheses carefully as more information comes in.

3.9 Teacher's books: Who needs/reads 'em?

Richard Sloane, *Cambridge Academy of English*

Although I have written a number of teacher's books (TBs) to go with students' coursebooks over the years, I have not seen much debate on the usefulness (or otherwise) of TBs. So, when Felicity O'Dell in Cambridge started a debate on the Internet via TESL-L last year, I asked her to forward all the messages she got to me, and these formed the core of the data I used in my talk.

Interestingly, most of the respondents, who came from many different countries, said that, while they themselves were greatly in favour of TBs, they believed that most of their colleagues did not bother much with them.

Many good reasons were suggested for using TBs, the most fundamental of which were that they saved teachers time in lesson preparation and that they gave teachers additional ideas for spicing up their lessons.

However, many reasons were also suggested for why teachers were not in favour of them. The main ones would seem to be that they often just give the answers to exercises in the SB with limited guidance and methodological help. Format problems were also mentioned: they are frequently too dense, not clearly laid out and too heavy to carry around. One interesting point which the audience agreed with was that the RSA Cert and Trinity courses placed too much emphasis on teachers creating their own materials and not enough on how to work effectively with coursebooks.

The last part of the talk concerned what the ideal TB might look like. Many suggestions were made. I have divided these into content and format possibilities.

Content possibilities included:

- have them more like a teacher's resource book, with photocopiable worksheets and ideas which can be adapted immediately;
- include a lot of extra discussion and writing topics to make students think about topics related to the themes, i.e. spinning off beyond the SB;
- include, for example, grammar games related to the topics and sample tests;
- point out tricky grammar, false friends and anything else that might pose problems for the students.

Format possibilities included:

- make them interleaved with the SB (like the *Cambridge English Course*);
- make them slightly larger than the SB with the SB pages reproduced and minimised, and in the big margins around the edges add the methodological suggestions, etc.
- put them into loose-leaf binders so that pages can be removed and added at will.

The audience agreed that there were practical problems associated with many of the suggestions. I also pointed out that publishers tend to want TBs to be as cheap as possible as they never make a profit and that this would inevitably influence the adoption of some of these ideas. But there seemed to be general agreement amongst the small but enthusiastic audience that TBs do need another look at. There were a number of publishers at the presentation, all of whom said that they would be examining their TBs again in the light of the talk.

3.10 'Shorts'

Modifying a spoken English course through student feedback, *Aysegul Daloglu, Middle East Technical University, Ankara*

In addition to identifying specific needs, this questionnaire also identified the topics the students wanted to focus on in the lessons. The most frequently mentioned topic was focusing on daily events and interesting topics. The second most frequently mentioned area was talking about personal experiences. Philosophy and extraordinary events were the third most popular areas that could be focused on in the lessons. In addition to these, their responses indicated that they did not want to focus on topics related to pollution, smoking, and life in our solar system as these issues were extensively discussed in their earlier studies.

Teaching young learners of EFL through songs, dances and games, *Leonora Fröhlich-Ward, University of Munich*

The Peg game

Divide the class into two teams. The children of Team A write their names in washable ink on the flat part of plastic pegs. You pin one peg on the back of each child, making sure that no child has its own name on its back. Each child from Team B picks a 'pegged' partner from Team A and reads the name on his/her back. Child A has to find out who he/she is by asking the questions *Am I a boy/girl? Have I got a blue pullover? Is my name Peter?* At the end of a given time the number of children who have found out what name is on their backs is marked on the board. The game is repeated with Team B being 'pegged' and having to ask the questions about themselves. The element of competition encourages the answering team only to accept English questions, which turns this into effective learning.

Storytelling/listening

We listened to a story – *Goldilocks* – and had great fun! Every participant had a word to listen for and had to stand up whenever it was mentioned in the story. There were lots of 'ups and downs'.

Setting up a literature course for non-specialists, *Philip Minkoff, Nantes Atlantic Graduate School of Management*

A literary narrative yields meaning in three ways:

- Story: What does the story tell? Setting, characters, events/plot.
- Text: How does the text tell the story? Vocabulary and grammar, discourse structure, textual time and space, parallelisms, etc.
- Narration: How do the narrator and reader give meaning to the story? Narrative voice, point of view, reader response, etc.

All three ways should be explored because the overall meaning depends on all three.

The second part of the presentation dealt with the approach taken to A S Byatt's short story *The Chinese Lobster*. The order in which these elements are discussed matters little, and this particular text, with its extraordinary textual and narrative wealth, can be approached from any angle. The brainstorming question *What's the text about?* produces the following suggestions: seafood, the impossibility of communication, anorexia/depression, the nature of art, sexual harassment, suicide, hedonism, epicureanism, existentialism. The challenge is to explore each of these ideas and discover links between them (the links are very tight). A discussion of the vocabulary draws students' attention to the subtleties of colour and texture which, in turn, link in with the themes identified by the students.

Similarly, the unusual grammar, especially in the early description of the lobster, is a useful clue in discovering and creating meanings. The many metaphors and fractured symmetries can be identified and discussed, leading students to a general awareness of the story's cohesiveness and its underlying philosophical and aesthetic assumptions.

A phonetician's view of readings from literature, *Olga Mindrul, Moscow State University*

In pronunciation teaching today there is as much concern with suprasegmental or prosodic features as with articulation of vowels and consonants. From teaching sound drills, phoneticians have gradually moved to teaching intonation in communicative contexts and are now showing a growing interest in investigation and teaching of such general features as *setting* and *voice quality*.

... It is for that reason that recordings of literary texts are invaluable: the feelings, emotions and attitudes expressed in them are not abstract or stripped of the context or situation. The listeners possess full background knowledge provided by the context of the story or novel, or play. They do not have to analyse sentences taken out of context and pronounced by someone in a simulated situation; they become emotionally involved in the development of the story and are sensitive to all the nuances of characters' speech.

Working with literature, *Sandy Kennedy, Chichester Institute of Higher Education*

The Shakespearean sonnet *The Seven Ages of Man* provided the basis for investigations into specific linguistic features and interaction strategies for each of the seven stages. The students drew on a rich variety of sources – books, magazines, films, videos and personal observations (often recorded), and came up with findings and observations which were informed and sensitive, revealing a depth of study that had not been expected or even asked for.

The scheme below outlines how the programme was conducted:

- highlighting the quotations (e.g. *at first the infant mewling and puking in his nurse's arms*); discussing unfamiliar words and phrases;
- brainstorming for ideas: e.g. 'When I say the word *baby*, what do you see, hear, feel, think?' Eliciting further lexis by association;
- research: reading around the topic, interviewing, filming and recording, selecting data for presentation, including published poems, composing a poem;
- reporting back to the class, reading poems aloud, discussing reasons for writing the poems, arranging data collection, peer and tutor reading and correction;
- mounting a poster display; compilation of a book;
- preparing a conference paper and assisting with the supporting video.

Monolingual vs semi-bilingual dictionaries, *Lionel Kenerman, ELT Consultant, Tel Aviv*

The innovators of the monolingual learner's dictionary, Michael West and A S Hornby, and their successors, brought ELT a big step forward. But they also took it one step backwards. They wanted students to think in English when using a dictionary. But by eliminating translations entirely, they threw out the baby with the bath water. The mother tongue point-of-reference was gone. Gone was the reassurance of knowing that a word was correctly understood. And gone was the satisfaction derived from finding out the meanings of new words in the mother tongue. Frustration and uncertainty reign in a learner's mind when the search for the L1 equivalent is not satisfied. No wonder learners continued to use at home (and under their desks) their well-thumbed bilingual dictionaries. And no wonder that monolingual learners' dictionaries quickly caught on with teachers.

Monolingual learners' dictionaries encourage thinking in L1, have examples, have explanations about usage, and are not ambiguous. But they contain too much information, are exceedingly complicated to use, are culturally biased, and do not satisfy the need for translations. Semi-bilingual dictionaries, on the other hand, reinforce correct understanding, reveal misunderstandings and rectify them, satisfy the psychological need to know the L1 equivalent, are user-friendly and learner-friendly, and make for cultural balance.

4 THE NEW TECHNOLOGIES

4.1 Using Internet for communicative practice

Aldo M Higashi, *Universidad Catolica del Peru*

Modern ELT methodology aims to develop the students' communicative skills. Most classroom activities are designed so students can learn and practise new language by exchanging information about themselves and their world. Additionally, textbooks include a series of information-gap activities which will help them acquire new language in a realistic way.

At the same time, computers have become important tools in modern life. They are now used in almost every aspect of life, and second language teaching is no exception. However, most of the excellent programs available provide guided student-computer interaction which is useful for practising grammar, functions and even lexical items but not for real communication. Besides, if you make a typing mistake or enter an unexpected response, the computer will consider your answer wrong even if it is communicatively right. Fortunately, the Internet offers services for using computers as channels for student-student interaction.

One of these services is MOOing. MOOs are virtual places where users from all over the world communicate and collaborate with other users at the same time and in different rooms. MOOs can be accessed using telnet or MOO clients like *Zmud*. A useful MOO for students of English is *schMOOze University* (Telnet *schmooze.hunter.cuny.edu 8888*). Once you log on, follow the instructions on screen and go directly to the classrooms to learn the basic commands. However, you can start communicating with others by starting your messages with opening quotations, like 'Hello'. *SchMOOze* provides many tools to help students communicate, like a campus map, dictionaries, a thesaurus, and an encyclopedia. It also helps them with conversion tools for temperature and time zones.

Now that browsers have become so popular, you can also use them for chatting after installing the corresponding plug-in, which can be downloaded the first time you connect to a chat site. You can check the sites available at *http//www.ichat.com.* I recommend *Open24* (*http://chat.open24.net:4080*).

For faster connections and computers you can also try 3D sites or 'virtual worlds' which add the visual element. This makes communication more realistic and motivating. Besides, students learn some of the extra-linguistic aspects of language, like keeping the correct distance between two speakers. One of these sites, *Worlds Chat*, can be accessed with software you download from *http://www.worlds.net.* The other, *Cyberhub*, is accessed with your browser and a plug-in at *http//www.blacksun.com.* Both of these places allow students to see the other participants before they start talking to them, as well as walking around and getting to know the rooms and areas of each site.

These virtual places can be used for practising English in many imaginative ways. For instance, you can have beginners interview other students about their countries, occupations, addresses, etc. Intermediate students can be assigned more elaborate tasks, like doing some research on a topic which requires getting information from other students in various parts of the world.

If you'd like more detailed information, e-mail me at *ahigash@pucp.edu.pe*

4.2 Interactive exercises for language learning on the Internet

Peter Biddulph, *Freelance*

The Internet, and in particular the World Wide Web, is an ideal environment for the creation and dissemination of interactive language materials since the exercises are accessible worldwide, and the supporting programs run on almost any computer. Using the familiar medium of the WWW, the exercises present examples of language from authentic contexts, evaluate a user's input and provide feedback. Students respond by selecting from a list of words and phrases, or by entering text. Many of the exercises accept either form of response: students may try an exercise with the words displayed, before testing themselves by entering their own text.

The operation and feedback mechanisms are simple and consistent: when the correct selection is made, the target word or phrase is printed to the page and the input device (list box, radio button or text box) is removed; otherwise the input device remains.

Examples implementing types of exercise found in the Cambridge Examinations and in course books were presented to familiarise the audience with the mechanisms involved and highlight the underlying aims. *The Quiz on The Arts* consists of sentences each 'chunked' into three parts: the work of art, the verb phrase and the agent (artist). For example,

'Psycho'
[was painted by] [George Orwell]
[was directed by] [David Hockney]
[was written by] [Alfred Hitchcock].

The students compose sentences rather than simply selecting the right answer to a question. Exercises on multi-word verbs, reporting verbs, and a text to practise editing skills concluded this section.

The Sick Lion, a fable by Aesop, formed the basis for the next exercises.

Reading comprehension

Construction of sentences paraphrasing the original text. For example,

The lion couldn't	*[go into]*	*[for the lion]*
The beasts felt	*[hunt]*	*[the lion's den]*
The fox wouldn't	*[sorry]*	*[for food]*

The lion couldn't hunt for food paraphrases the original 'The lion was unable to provide himself with food by force'.

Word search exercise

A number of words and phrases are given (*ate*, *decided*, etc.). The students have to type in a word similar in meaning from the text ('devoured', 'resolved', etc.).

Four exercises on linking words and phrases

The students are presented with example sentences, and then directed to a series of increasingly challenging exercises in which the focus shifts from comprehension and recognition to composition and use.

1 Match sentence halves where one half contains a linking word or phrase.
2 Select the appropriate linking word or phrase to complete the sentences.
3 Select the appropriate linking word and sentence 'tail'.
4 Students type in their own words to complete the sentences.

Contextual cues in the first exercise help the students to match the two halves while familiarising them with the linking devices. The next two exercises test the students' ability to use an appropriate linking phrase. The last, free practice, exercise requires moderation. In this instance the completed exercise is forwarded to the teacher via e-mail.

Finally, an authoring program was demonstrated. Teachers and students can create their own gap-fill exercises online from anywhere in the world. After entering their text, the mouse is used to select words or phrases to gap.

Try out the exercises at *http://www.point2.co.uk/lnet/*

Correspondence address: *68 Colwyn House, Hercules Road, London SE1 7DA, UK*

4.3 *Merlin* – EFL on the Internet

Imogen Arnold, Nicolette Ellis, Julian Halliwell and Debra Marsh, *University of Hull*

Merlin (Multimedia Educational Research into Learning via an Information Network) is a distance learning environment developed collaboratively by the University of Hull Language Institute and BT Research Laboratories. Since development began in September 1995, the objective has been to address the needs of learners and teachers of languages in particular. Whilst offering flexibility of time, place and pace, the emphasis has been on:

- providing for interaction and collaboration in order to foster the rapport characteristic of classroom learning;
- generating language use which is authentic to learners;
- supporting independent learning;
- providing pedagogically sound materials tailorable to differing needs;
- balancing development across the four skills.

The backbone of *Merlin* is two existing global networks – the Internet and the telephone system, integrated using the *Rise* (Real-time Interactive Social Environment) platform, and accessed using a web browser. Following two trials of the platform and its application to EFL learning, *Merlin Intermediate English* is the first complete course to use the *Merlin* environment, running in the first instance for 15 weeks from March to July 1997, with one tutor and 35 learners located in 17 different countries.

This course is structured around the *Pathway* – a task-based syllabus, within which the tutor selects language practice activities from a resource bank. Through emphasis on collaboration, the *Pathway* focuses usage of the surrounding resources and interactional facilities. These are:

- *The Meeting Place*: a forum for spoken interaction enabling members of the group to view who is currently on-line, instigate or join group and pair audio-conferences, share and discuss Internet sites during audio-conferences, make individual recordings or recordings of pair and group conversations.
- *The Portfolio*: a searchable database for storing and retrieving written and spoken work completed during the course, as well as written or spoken messages sent to others. *The Portfolio* holds both a group workbook accessible to all students for comment and comparison, and the personal workbooks of each student, visible only to that student and the tutor.
- *A tutor notice-board* for posting course information and links to relevant external web sites used in supplementary tasks.
- *A diary* which adapts to the local time of each user: for learners to coordinate their sessions on-line and plan their time in advance.
- *The Resource Centre*: providing learning material to supplement that selected for the *Pathway*; guided access to external web sites; learning to learn advice; and *Laureate* – a facility for converting written text into sound files.
- *A Merlin homepage* for each member of the group.
- *A written conferencing facility* for messages sent between individuals,

and to conference areas accessible to the whole group.

For up-to-date information on *Merlin*, see *http://www.hull.ac.uk/langinst/merlin*

4.4 Business English on the Web

Duncan Baker, *Lydbury English Centre*

Some advantages of using the Web as a Business English resource:

- WWW provides an immediately available and up-to-date business resource;
- it can easily be downloaded and tailored for individual needs;
- it is 'pulled' information and not 'pushed';
- it is genuinely authentic material and not tailored for the EFL market;
- it appeals to those who are used to using such resources in their daily lives.

Sample simulations

Report writing

Construct the bare bones of a report comparing and contrasting two or three of the oil companies from their web site information. The report is intended to be presented to potential investors in the oil industry.

Presentation skills

Using similar information, prepare a short presentation describing the market and trading situation of one of the premier oil companies. The object of this presentation will be a PR company you are considering employing to represent you.

Project and product management

You are a consultancy presenting a possible PR campaign for one of the major oil companies which has recently been accused of allowing pollution to escape from one of its drilling platforms.

Some initial reference points

The public records office
http://www.open.gov.uk/pro/prohome.htm

The Financial Times *http://www.ft.com*

Business daily newspaper
http://www.clickit.com/touch/newpage.htm

Financial Times company briefing page
http://www.ft.com/cgi-bin/pft/ftcdbdb/fti.d2w/report/

British Petroleum
http://www.bp.com/bp2.html

Shell Oil Company
http://www.shellus.com/

American Oil Company
http://www.amoco.com

Burmah Castrol
http://www.foseco.com/parent.htm

Information gathering and fax/e-mail drafting

You are the PA to the training manager of a large oil company based in London. You have four delegates coming to a meeting in London next Wednesday starting at 11.00. The delegates are coming from Telford, Plymouth, Frankfurt and Aberdeen. Find the best travel plan for each delegate and draft a fax or e-mail to each of them outlining their recommended method of travel. The delegates wish to spend the minimum amount of time away from home.

Some initial reference points

Train times
http://www.railtrack.co.uk/travel/

British Airways
http://www.british-airways.com

Lufthansa
http://www.lufthansa.co.uk/home.html

4.5 Using presentation software in Business English training

Patricia Brooks, *Cambridge Centre for Languages*

Presentation software allows speakers to build their presentation slides on computer within the pre-formatted structure of templates.

Benefits to Business English training

Structure and visuals

The client provides the trainer with a summary of the message. Together they map out a coherent progression from one point to the next. The templates help to break down a complex message into manageable chunks. The slides provide anchor points for the presenter and for the audience.

Language training

The trainer can then help to adjust or feed in any language as appropriate, and can work on problems highlighted on the presentation slides and in the supporting material to develop clarity of language and an effective delivery style. Most importantly, there is more time to practise the delivery. The more secure the client feels about the preparation, the more confident the delivery will be and the more effective the message.

Confidence

We know that confidence is a crucial element in second language learning. The degree of success the client has in acquiring the tools he or she needs to perform in the second language depends greatly on how soon the positive cycle of learning can be engaged. This is doubly relevant in presentation training, and presentation software can help here.

Presentation software as CALL?

The benefits of using CALL are most obvious when the program makes language processing routine (editing, recycling). The program enhances learner-centredness (task-based learning focused on specific needs), and the acquisition of a useful computer skill enhances motivation (presentation software is widely used in business).

Why is presentation software is so popular in the business world?

- it's easy to use;
- it's convenient: *PowerPoint* allows for the integration of material from other *Microsoft* applications;
- it's flexible: presentations can be changed or recycled for different situations and it suits horizontal management structures – teams can collaborate on presentation structure and content on the company network;
- it's much cheaper than the alternative of having slides made by an outside bureau.

Fitting presentation software into a course programme

Use of presentation software can be included in the training course at micro task level leading on to the final product as illustrated in the micro-macro framework outlined by Peter Shaw in *ESP SIG Newsletter* No 5 Feb 1996. The client can also work on *PowerPoint* in self-access.

To sum up

Presentation software can help trainers and in-service clients to make and give better presentations because the templates help structure the message; it provides high quality visual support; efficient organisation of the message means more time for improving language and practising delivery; thorough preparation using current business software builds confidence.

4.6 Now let's use it – integrating multimedia into the language classroom

Roberta Stock and Miriam Schcolnik, *Tel Aviv University*

Selection of appropriate multimedia depends on projected use: as curriculum provider, as specific skill builder or as enrichment.

Types of programs

- edutainment: combines entertainment and education
- instructional programs: teach and test
- general reference: for example, dictionaries and encyclopedias
- specific resources: focus on specific subjects or topics (the human heart, etc.)
- authoring programs: allow development of customised multimedia lessons
- task-based programs: students learn while performing a task.

Uses

- complete curriculum: software packages covering a whole curriculum such as *Nieuwe Buren*, a complete course of Dutch as a second language, and *The Q Kit*, a complete course for young EFL beginners
- class supplement: regardless of depth and focus, almost any program can be used to add variety to the course
- 'rainy day' enrichment: sporadic use
- review: the program reinforces what was presented in class
- remediation: helps students bridge gaps; often based on diagnostic testing.

The potential user judges the suitability of the program to his/her educational philosophy and teaching approach, the learner's needs and background, and the syllabus. A simple checklist may prove useful: based on sound pedagogical principles; clear objectives; learner control; true interaction; on-line tools; clear, varied choices; easy to use; appropriate to learners' background and needs; relevant and meaningful to the learner; enjoyable and motivational; appropriate for different learning styles; assessment tools; teacher utilities; encourages thinking; conforms to multimedia standards; clear, on-line help; good technical manual; other resource materials; part of a line of products.

Integrating multimedia programs into the language classroom

Programs covering a whole curriculum may also be used at certain points in the course for specific purposes. However, programs covering certain aspects of the syllabus can only be used as complementary. Integration activities can be devised for any program. Multimedia programs are more effective when integrated into the course, when the computer session is not an isolated event.

4.7 CD-ROM: The flexible textbook

Diana Lindsay, *Federation of Basque Schools*

Is there a way of providing teachers with a wealth of curriculum design, teaching guidelines and materials without forcing them to follow the limited and linear proposals of a textbook? This presentation demonstrated the work done by a European team led from the Basque Country, working with a *Socrates* grant on materials for teaching English as a foreign language (with Italian, Dutch and Spanish to follow).

The flexibility of the CD-ROM suits the needs of the team. The material can be easily adapted to the local setting and curriculum demands. More material can be added and changes made as teachers try it out and improve or add to it. The CD-ROM is also very cheap to produce.

The CD-ROM presented at IATEFL has two components: an Electronic Book with ten Story Projects for 8 to 10-year-olds and an Activity Bank, which allows for a freer access to all the activities collected. Two sets of activities are provided for each Story Project. The first set relate directly to the story: dramatising the story, telling the story with the storybook, singing the song, oral and written games and vocabulary games with flashcards. The CD-ROM contains the drama scripts, the storybooks, the song scripts and music (also on audio cassette), flashcards, activity descriptions with contents and procedure, assessment tools and resource lists. A second set of more general activities are also included, which relate to topics that arise in the stories.

The Activity Bank collects together all the activities developed for the Story Projects (about 300 so far) and will be added to as partner countries add variations and new activities. The bank allows free access to all the activities independently of the Story Projects. By using a series of descriptors (*topic*, *type*, *skill*, *interaction*, etc.) teachers are able to search for and print activities that interest them most and suit their needs.

There is no doubt that the CD-ROM has an extraordinary capacity to store a great deal of material for the teacher in a very compact and economical way. For the teacher who prefers not to work within the limited confines of a textbook but does not have time to look through an ever increasing number of teachers' handbooks and resource books, the CD-ROM offers a flexible tool for storing teachers' materials, and all at the click of a mouse.

4.8 'Shorts'

Cyberspace and silver disks are texts (1), *Susan Diane Mace, Britannia Schools, Brazil*

One of the big hits amongst students (and those who attended this presentation) was the use of trailers of films about to open, downloaded from the Internet site *http://www.hollywood.com* and the flavour of real-world interactivity offered by sites such as the *FBI 10 most wanted criminals* – as well as the combined use of CD-ROM multimedia reference texts with potential Internet follow-up work or vice versa.

Samples of work and handouts are available at our site: *http://www.britannia.com.br*

How to implement a multimedia course effectively, *Harriet Seymour, Interactive Language Teaching*

There are two obvious methods for using multimedia. You can either use the multimedia course as the curriculum and consolidate what is taught on the screen in the teacher contact time, or you can use the multimedia course to consolidate what is taught in the classroom. For the first, you need to establish an effective ratio between self study and teacher contact time.

... A student tracking programme is important to record progress. You should ask what information it is giving and how useful it is. Some programs give an assessment. The danger is that the software is setting the agenda.

Multimedia: Personal choice, personal response, *Rhiannon Williams, Eurocentre Cambridge*

This talk argued that multimedia is ideally suited to stimulating language acquisition through training the user to make choices in learning and through its power to evoke emotion.

As changing one's learning style is deeply personal, learner independence is rarely achieved when working in a classroom setting where individual training needs cannot be dealt with in depth, or with printed self-access material which offers little support, engagement or flexibility.

The use of multimedia is essentially a process of making choices – of route through the material, of modality (visual, textual, aural) and whether to go for overview or concentrate on detail. It is a natural environment in which to offer an experience of a variety of learning styles and options.

Multimedia has derived its structural language from television and cinema as well as games. Our willingness to experience emotions in the privacy of viewing or playing enables language to be processed at a deeper cognitive level.

Multimedia enables users to take more control over their learning as they become more confident of their needs by offering a combination of tools (such as interactive reference works) and material (vast banks of texts) which can be recombined with each other or with resources from the wider world.

Cyberspace and silver disks are texts (2), *Susan Diane Mace, Britannia Schools, Brazil*

In a few years, even conference proceedings may well be a virtual summary that you can see, watch, hear and listen to – while you read, interact, query or download, change, and make your own, if you like. Because that is what all this is about – making our teaching and learning texts 'live'.

5 LANGUAGE AND LANGUAGE TEACHING

5.1 Plenary: Lost nails and maypoles – some current language issues

Jean Aitchison, *University of Oxford*

Lost nails are topics that currently worry people, split here into 'lost nails' and 'bizarre behaviour'. *Maypoles* are questions at the forefront of recent research, subdivided into 'maypoles' and 'absolute disasters'.

Lost nails: cultural models

'Lost nails' is about linguachondria – my label for 'language hypochondria'. Linguachondriacs believe that English is crumbling into dust, and lament the supposed lack of care which is bringing this about. If speakers are careless over language details, then the whole linguistic edifice may collapse, they assume, just as a lost nail may entail a lost horseshoe, a lost horse, then a lost rider:

> Taking the easy way out is now the norm. We shall by the year 2150 or thereabouts, have come full circle. Clawing our way painfully and slowly from Neanderthal grunting ... we shall descend swiftly to Neanderthal grunting again. What a waste! Yours frustratedly ...

This letter was one of several similar ones which I received after my 1996 BBC Reith lectures, where I had argued that we need to understand language, not try to control it (Aitchison, 1997). According to these pessimistic correspondents, strenuous efforts are required to preserve our language, and prevent its disintegration.

To anyone professionally concerned with language, this view seems weird. Yet English teachers need to be aware of cultural models, and how they arose: learners might encounter this 'lost nail' view, and wonder how to handle it.

The 'lost nail' model is an inherited one. Eighteenth century anxieties over the apparent fluidity of English changed into nineteenth century worries about decay. Foremost among the worriers was an influential Archbishop of Dublin, Richard Chevenix Trench (Crowley 1989), who promoted his bizarre belief that the language of 'savage tribes' had slithered down from former excellence:

> What does their language on close inspection prove? In every case what they are themselves, the remnant and ruin of a better and a nobler past. Fearful indeed is the impress of degradation which is stamped on the language of the savage (Trench 1851, in Harris 1996)

Trench regarded language as a 'moral barometer', and assumed that 'with every impoverishing or debasing of personal or national life goes hand in hand a corresponding impoverishment and debasement of language'. As evidence of this 'degradation', he quotes a missionary who worked in Africa, among the

Bechuanas who supposedly had lost the word for 'a supreme Divine Being':

> ... so there is nothing that so effectually tends to keep him in the depths to which he has fallen ... Thus ... the very terms are well nigh or wholly wanting in the dialect of the savage whereby to impart to him heavenly truths

In short, Trench promoted three bizarre false views: first, that language and morals are somehow intertwined; second, that languages may disintegrate; third, that vigilance is needed to prevent linguistic collapse. As a result, generations of learners have been instructed to curl their linguistic eyelashes, and pluck their linguistic eyebrows, as it were: to pay attention to details, often quite irrelevant ones, such as 'Don't split infinitives' – a prohibition invented by 18th century purists.

But language mends its own patterns and keeps itself in check: it works more like a thermostat than a nail in a horseshoe. Fears for its safety are unnecessary. But awareness of linguachondria – and its causes – is useful for language teachers.

Bizarre behaviour: communicative competence

Her uncle's gone bananas; Her uncle is exhibiting bizarre behaviour; Her uncle is mentally challenged – Which, if any, should be used when? How is a learner or teacher to distinguish between gobbledygook, 'political correctness', and ordinary usage? Such communicative competence is the goal of many learners.

A first distinction is between technical terminology and gobbledygook. Technical terminology is not gobbledygook, though it becomes so if used inappropriately among non-specialists (Aitchison, 1986, 1997). This often occurs with legal language, when a document which needs to be understood by the general public is written in terms which only lawyers understand. At that point it becomes inappropriate, as in some insurance policies:

> Whereas the Insured herein named has by a signed proposal and declaration dated as herein stated which proposal and declaration the Insured has agreed shall be the basis of this Contract and be held as incorporated herein ... (Plain English Campaign, 1994)

A second contrast is between euphemism and political correctness – though here the borderline is fuzzy. Euphemisms are an essential part of life: it is more tactful to say someone is *mentally challenged* than *mad* (Ayto, 1993). But there is more to it than tact. And this is where recent linguistic corpora – databases which provide multiple real examples of words in context – become an essential tool. They enable teachers and learners to distinguish the various uses.

An examination of terms relating to mental health in a corpus of mainly newspaper language indicates that terms sometimes labelled 'politically correct' (PC) fall into several categories. One is jokes:

Are some backbenchers too ***intellectually challenged*** *to be MPs at all?*

But mostly they reflect formal rather than informal language:

People who are physically or ***mentally challenged*** *are part of life.*

These terms overlap with technical jargon: *mentally disturbed* is standard formal 'psychiatry speak':

Mental health charities have drawn public attention to the plight of ***mentally disturbed*** *people inappropriately contained in prisons.*

So also is *bizarre behaviour:* it characterises someone who is assumed to be mentally ill, but whose specific illness has not yet been diagnosed:

an entire pattern of psychotic symptoms that is recognized as schizophrenia if a man shows ***bizarre behaviour****, delusions, hallucinations*

These semi-formal, written terms contrast with informal descriptions, such as *bonkers*, *bananas*, and *nuts*, found in some newspapers, and also spoken speech:

Has the market gone ***bonkers****?*
Spiders send me ***bananas***
It drives you ***nuts****.*

And a recent fashionable, colloquial way of expressing bizarre behaviour is the phrase: *Two sandwiches short of a picnic*. On accessing the words *short of* in a corpus, it becomes clear that this is currently giving rise to a plethora of offshoots:

He's two cans short of a six-pack
Gina was two clean napkins short of a picnic basket
Three anchovies short of a pizza.

To summarise, anyone teaching or learning English needs to sort out gobbledygook from technical terminology, and formal from informal language. Dismissing the whole PC movement misses the point. No easy answers exist: the evidence for each term has to be sifted. Linguistic corpora enable teachers and learners to do this, and also to chart the rise and fall of vogue phrases.

So far, questions which worry people have been discussed. In what follows, current research issues will be outlined. These have been subdivided into 'maypoles' and 'absolute disasters'.

Maypoles: verb structures

Verbs are the maypole around which the sentence revolves, and they determine its structure. The maypole behaviour of verbs has become increasingly important in modern research on the lexicon, and provides a key to proficiency for learners (Aitchison, 1994).

Traditionally, verbs are divided into those without an object (intransitive) as in *Pauline coughed*, and those with an object (transitive), as in *Paul caught a fish*. But this is a vast oversimplification, and verb structures are considerably more subtle. A verb such as *creep* requires more information than the simple label 'intransitive': *Lionel crept* is incomplete, and needs an additional preposition phrase, as in *Lionel crept down the hall. Mavis put the goldfish* is similarly incomplete: the location has to be specified, as in *Mavis put the goldfish in the bath*.

This is still not the whole story. Clumps of verbs with a similar meaning tend to cluster together in their syntactic behaviour (Levin, 1993). Sound emission verbs have the source of sound followed by the sound emitted: *the bell clanged*; *the siren wailed*. Light emission words follow a similar pattern: *the lightning flashed*; *the sun shone*.

Some verb patterns can be deceptive. Take 'grooming' verbs, such as *shower, wash*. These may be intransitive, as in *Tim showered*; *Helen washed*, in which case Tim and Helen are grooming themselves. If they are grooming someone else, then the groomed object is specified: *Tim showered the dog*; *Helen washed the baby*. But 'activity' verbs, such as *cook* and *clean* pattern differently. *Don cooked*; *Angela cleaned* does not mean that Don and Angela are cooking or cleaning themselves: the object is assumed to be something external and inanimate, as *Don cooked the dinner*; *Angela cleaned the floor*.

English speakers know these patterns intuitively, and are often surprised when the difference between *wash* and *clean* is pointed out. But they probably acquired these patterns as children, by paying attention to the words which surrounded the verb.

Sensitivity to the surrounding words is now thought to be the key to learning grammatical rules. Humans acquire the maypole alongside its attached strands. They are supersensitive to words which occur together. But this supersensitivity has further implications, as will be discussed below.

Absolute disasters

Collocation (words which are located next to one another) and co-occurrence (words which occur near one another) are of major importance in language learning. For example, antonyms (opposites) are probably learned because they tend to occur near one another:

Don't mix ***clean*** *clothes with* ***dirty*** *ones*
You'll have to take the ***rough*** *with the* ***smooth***

and so on (Fellbaum, 1995).

Noticing which words occur together is a natural human talent, the key to sounding like a native speaker. Indeed, at the origin of language around 100,000 years ago, habitual co-occurrence may have been how 'rules' became established in the first place (Aitchison, 1996).

Humans learn how to handle new words by paying attention to the other words around, as with *wimp*. This word is widely used, but it has crept into dictionaries only recently, so must have been learned via its use. In a survey of *wimp*-words in newspapers (Aitchison & Lewis, 1995), 65% of wimps were male, 2% were female, and the remainder were unspecified for sex. 84% were accompanied by clues to the pathetic nature of wimps. The word's negative image was specified either by its collocation with pejorative words, as *feeble wimp*; *dithering wimp*; *nervous wimp*, or by contrast with a positive image:

He was a go-getter, a doer, not some depressed wimp

or via a covert negative evaluation:

Who needs an enclosed cockpit? Wimps, that's who.

Co-occurrence is also the key to distinguishing near synonyms, such as *broad* and *wide*, *chase* and *pursue* – something which can puzzle foreign learners, because dictionaries often give similar definitions. Linguistic corpora can solve the puzzle of how English speakers manage to use them appropriately (Aitchison & Lewis, 1996). The examples below are speech from the British National Corpus, a database which includes both spoken and written English.

Wide and *broad* occasionally overlap, but mostly they are used in different contexts. *Wide* is predominantly used in measurements, where it tends to co-occur with *long* and *deep*:

The dish is about this ***long****, this* ***wide****, and about that* ***deep****. And I make it on Thursdays, nice big lasagna. And I ate it all!*

Broad, on the other hand, is mainly used to mean 'lacking detail'. It occurs in phrases such as *broad outline*; *broad spectrum*; *broad sweep*; *broad terms*:

*In **broad terms** the master plan is unchanged in concept but we think improved in detail.*

Chase and *pursue* are also distinguished by their contexts. English speakers use them with different objects, even though they might not consciously realise it. We *chase* runaway horses, burglars, balls and other physical things, as in *More frigging football! Bunch of tarts going round a field **chasing** a ball!* But we *pursue* abstract ideas, aims, targets, and policies, as in: *We need to take the initiative in **pursuing** a strategy for employment and growth.* So footballs are not normally *pursued*, nor are targets *chased*, even though the meaning 'follow after' is given for both *chase* and *pursue* in some dictionaries.

'Bleached' words (Aitchison & Lewis, in prep) represent another problem for learners. These are words whose meaning is a pale shade of what it once was:

*I was **devastated** when Sainsbury's discontinued Nature's Compliments hand and body cream in Vanilla fragrance*

ran a recent letter to a newspaper. This seems odd for a discontinued beauty product, at least when compared with some dictionary definitions. A learner who consulted, say, *The Longman Dictionary of the English Language* (1991 edition) would find that *devastate* was 'to reduce to ruin; lay waste; to have a shattering effect on; overwhelm'. The difficulty for learners is that old and new senses co-exist, often for quite a long time. A customer *devastated* over unavailable hand-cream may occur alongside someone severely emotionally shocked:

Nick Pollard ... finished up dead after a street fight ... His family and friends are devastated.

Yet *prostrated by grief* is still pale when contrasted with the word's older, but still current meaning of 'laid waste' (of land):

*An area nearly twice the size of Belgium was **devastated**.*

Or take the word *tragedy*:

*The great **tragedy** of modern music is that ... the results are less and less significant from a human point of view*

wrote a musicologist. But modern music is hardly a catastrophe, at least when compared to a major air-crash:

*259 passengers and crew ... were killed by a bomb. This was Britain's worst air **tragedy**.*

And the actress who

*turns in a sharp cameo as the girl's, vulgar, port-tippling mother, a **disaster** area in fake leopard-skin and stacked heels*

is a long way from

*the Hillsborough football **disaster** which killed 95 people.*

Such variation illustrates the way language changes: variants creep in, they fluctuate and co-exist, then the newer usages may oust the old. Once again, the use of corpora enables multiple real usages to be studied within context and reduces the puzzle.

Words derived from the same base move apart at different speeds. Different word classes (parts of speech) behave independently, and show different levels of bleaching. The adjective/participle *devastated* often has a faded meaning: personal emotional disturbance accounts for over 50% of instances, as in:

Jackson sent a message to fans saying he was ***devastated*** *he was not able to do Saturday's show.*

Yet the unhappy state of mind of individuals is unlikely to be one of true *devastation*. This noun is still more usually found in an older, more 'coloured' and catastrophic sense (82% of occurrences):

A huge bomb exploded, causing widespread ***devastation****.*

Bleaching starts in particular contexts. Cookery is a common disaster area, and minor episodes rate this label:

The gravy's a ***disaster****. It's got too much fat in it.*
Stephanie likes cooking, I don't, not since my ***disaster*** *with the soup.*

On the other hand, the kitchen is not a tragedy zone: it would sound odd to talk of the gravy being a *tragedy*, unless someone was poisoned.

Flamboyant writing is typical of certain topics. Sports writers often behave like boisterous guests trying to liven up a dull party, and *disasters* and *tragedies* abound:

He calmly controlled the ball before lashing an angled drive past Neville Southall ... It was a ***tragedy*** *for Everton.*
The last wicket fell ... So it was another blackwash, another ***disaster*** *for England.*

But meaning and general context are not the whole story. Each of these words has its preferred collocations. Sufferers are *absolutely devastated*, not 'very devastated'. An event is a *real tragedy*, not a 'true tragedy'. A bad judgement can be a *recipe for disaster*, but not a 'menu for disaster'.

In some cases, words which collocate can signal whether the event is a genuine disaster or a social hiccup: the word *absolute* indicates a fairly trivial event:

The majority of dinners are very pleasant affairs, but some can be ***absolute disasters****.*

But when a geographical name occurs with the words *disaster* and *tragedy*, then a genuinely appalling event is referred to, and weakening of meaning is absent, as in *the Bradford football* ***disaster****; the Bethnal Green tube-station* ***tragedy****.*

Sometimes, a group of similar meaning words join in a collocation. The words *effect, result, consequence* and similar collocate with *devastating* in 31% of occurrences, as in *Railways had a* ***devastating effect*** *on the fauna of the regions they penetrated.*

Bleaching is normal change, but speeded up and foreshortened. It sheds light on general processes of change, which often take much longer. But looking at these bleached words with the aid of corpora enables anyone to handle the complexities of the language with greater proficiency, and to see that, taken context by context, the effect is interesting and useful, rather than mysterious.

Conclusion

Two types of language issue have been discussed – 'Lost nails', which looked at some current language worries, and 'maypoles', which outlined some recent research topics. For handling both types of issue, linguistic corpora provide an essential tool.

References

Aitchison J (1986) The gobbledygook syndrome *English Today* 5, 7–9

Aitchison J (1994) *Words in the Mind: An Introduction to the Mental Lexicon*, 2nd edition Oxford: Blackwell

Aitchison J (1996) *The Seeds of Speech: Language Origin and Evolution* Cambridge: Cambridge University Press

Aitchison J (1997) *The Language Web: The Power and Problem of Words* The 1996 BBC Reith lectures Cambridge: Cambridge University Press

Aitchison J & D M Lewis (1995) How to handle wimps: Incorporating new lexical items as an adult *Folia Linguistica* 29.1/2 7–20

Aitchison J & D M Lewis (1996) The mental word web: Forging the links In Svartvik J (Ed.) *Words* Stockholm: Swedish Academy 39–47

Aitchison J & D M Lewis (in prep) Absolute disasters and devastating effects: A study of bleaching

Ayto J (1993) *Euphemisms: Over 3,000 Ways to Avoid Being Rude or Giving Offence* London: Bloomsbury

Crowley T (1989) *The Politics of Discourse: The Standard Language Question in British Cultural Debates* London: Macmillan

Fellbaum C (1995) Co-occurrence and antonymy *International Journal of Lexicography* 8 281–303

Harris R (Ed.) (1996) *The Origin of Language* Bristol: Thoemmes Press

Levin B (1993) *English Verb Classes and Alternations: A Preliminary Investigation* Chicago: University of Chicago Press

Plain English Campaign (1994) *Utter Drivel! A Decade of Jargon and Gobbledygook* London: Robson

5.2 To split or to not split: A corpus-based typology of split infinitives

John Williams, *Cobuild*

Large corpora such as The Bank of English have given teachers and researchers the opportunity to revisit some of the old 'chestnuts' of English grammar, such as the split infinitive. Interestingly, it is difficult to find an authoritative 20th-century grammarian who outlaws this construction in all circumstances.

In the 323 million words of The Bank of English, there are 19,824 instances of the structure *to+[adverb]+[verb]*. The most frequent adverbs appearing between *to* and the verb are *just* (1,510 instances), *really* (1,466), *actually* (1,429), *further* (676), *even* (622), *fully* (511), *not* (491), *simply* (347), *better* (341), *finally* (330). This largely supports the view of Quirk, et al. (*A Comprehensive Grammar of the English Language* Longman 1985/1990) that the adverbials most likely to split the infinitive are 'subjuncts of narrow orientation' with a grading or emphasising function, or with a forward focus onto the following verb group. This leads us to the first category in our typology.

Type 1 Subjuncts of narrow orientation

the book 'How ***to really love*** *your child'*
It seemed undignified ***to even think*** *such a thing*

Further types are distinguished below. Naturally, some examples could fit into more than one category.

Type 2 Avoiding ambiguity or inappropriate emphasis

Students were asked ***to gradually assume*** *responsibility for performing the skill*
The government is paying workers compensation ***to partially offset*** *the new cost*

Type 3 Where the infinitive is followed by a lengthy object group

They have enabled him ***to specifically identify*** *the responses and physiological reactions that are essential to a sound marriage and those that can damage a relationship*

Type 4 In report structures

He confronted the two men and asked them ***to kindly leave*** *the house*
Tell them ***to always remember*** *that drill, even at traffic lights*

Type 5 Where the adverb and verb form a single semantic unit

a law that will make it illegal for bosses ***to sexually harass*** *their employees*
cities that they, in fact, want ***to ethnically cleanse***

Type 5a 'Positive negatives'

The women's movement has freed women ***to not have*** *children,* ***to not get*** *married, to be actresses, businesswomen and construction workers.*
We expect people here ***to not follow*** *the rules*

Type 6 'To boldly...'

Originating with the TV series *Star Trek*, this has 69 instances in The Bank of English, and has become a sort of icon of the split infinitive.

Star Trek is ***to boldly go*** *into a third series*
Publisher decides ***to boldly advocate*** *the split infinitive*

Type 7 With expletives

I need to know! I need ***to f***ing know!***

However, this type may not be a true split infinitive, as one can also split individual words with expletives as in *This is* ***un-f***ing-believable!***

5.3 The politics of determiners

Roger Berry, *Lingnan College, Hong Kong*

Determiners are in a very good position to manipulate impressions and attitudes since they precede nouns, which are the main content-givers in discourse; the very notion of *determining* implies this. The judicious use of determiners can lead to a very different interpretation on the part of listeners or readers, to make something seem positive or negative, significant or not, according to the wishes of speakers or writers. As Channell says 'native speakers ... recognise the inherent vagueness in non-numerical quantifiers and know how to exploit it for particular communicative purposes' (*Vague Language* OUP 1994:97). Here are some examples:

Manipulative *many*

On a number of occasions I have found myself using *many* (and *several*) when I had no idea, even vaguely, how many were involved. My sole purpose was to convey an impression of size to readers. Here is an example from an advert in a car magazine:

This year ***many*** *would-be Escort owners are opting for the stylish Kia Mentor hatchback.*

Clearly the producers have no evidence that the number involved is large or significant. The point is that in the same objective situation other people might use *some* or *a few*, but if these were used in the advert the whole point would be lost. This vagueness and potential for manipulation seems to me to be a central feature in the use of *many*.

Polite *any*

Because of its non-assertive nature, *any* is often used (even in positive sentences) when the speaker or writer wants to introduce an unpleasant topic, but without sounding impolite or threatening:

Any *praise may be deemed politically incorrect*

The proximity of a hedge in the shape of a modal verb is no coincidence; there is often a prosody of hypotheticality or tentativeness running through a whole clause. Determiners fulfil a similar function in noun phrases as modals do for verb phrases, and it is no accident that modals also come first in their respective phrase, where they have the greatest potential to orient the reader or listener towards the following head.

Derogatory *that*

The demonstratives have been well described in terms of time, space and textuality. What is often omitted is their emotive connotation. *That* is often associated with a derogatory comment; it may achieve this effect aided by a negative adjective or on its own:

That *stupid bus broke down not long after we left*
But what was Edwin doing bringing ***that*** *man along*

Distinctive *the*

Stressed *the* is often used as a way of expressing high praise:

This is ***THE*** *place to go*

Even when unstressed, *the* can be used to add distinction to something or someone, a point recognised by universities and other institutions when they insist on retaining the definite article at the start of their names (e.g. *The University of Hong Kong*).

Dismissive *some*

The use of stressed *some* can be a way for a speaker to show they hold someone or something to be of little importance:

They are having ***some*** *congressional meeting or something like that*

This is rather similar to derogatory *that*, except it involves indefinite reference.

5.4 Discovering grammar rules

Michael Swan and Catherine Walter, *Freelance*

Some learners seem to internalise grammar rules better when they have worked the rules out for themselves. This workshop aimed to help participants:

- assess the advantages and disadvantages of such an approach
- consider what types of input are most appropriate
- devise suitable exercises to guide learners in their discovery process.

One source of input for learner rule-making might be corpus data. But raw corpus data can be problematic: a sample of the British National Corpus entries with *became* demonstrated that short stretches of corpus data seldom incorporate their own context, and often contain cultural references that foreign learners may not recognise. Both these features make raw corpus data difficult for learners to handle.

Even tidied-up data can be hard to interpret without guidance. Participants spent a few minutes trying to derive rules about the use of *except* from a list of pairs of sentences.

Participants then discussed how they might make the rule-discovery process feasible and worthwhile for their learners. It was agreed that tidied-up data was most useful, but that it needed to be backed up by guidance. The following sorts of exercises were suggested (all examples from *How English Works* Swan & Walter OUP 1997):

Completing rules

- matching jumbled beginnings and endings of rules
- choosing the best ending for the beginning of a rule, from a list of possibilities.

Matching rules and forms

- after looking at examples, deciding which structure goes with which meaning
- looking at the examples and categorising them according to a set of questions. For example, after a set of examples of *make* and *do*: 'Do we use *do* or *make* to talk about work? Which do we use to talk about building and creating things?'

Choosing the best rule

For example, 'Look at the examples. Which of rules 1–5 gives the best explanation for the use of the past perfect?'

Directive questions

Giving examples and using questions to indicate the parameters of the rule/s. For example, a list of plurals and then a series of questions beginning 'What is the most common way of making the plurals of nouns? How do we make the plurals of words ending in *vowel + y*?'

Thinking out and drafting rules

This usually consists of a series of guided steps designed to show the learners what the parameters of the rule are, and ending with their writing a rule (probably in their own language, at least until a fairly advanced level).

It was agreed that different techniques would work for different structures and that it was important to match the difficulty of the rule to the technique chosen. It was also pointed out how important it was to provide an escape route for students who do not feel comfortable with this approach and will learn better if the rule is given to them from the beginning.

5.5 Plenary: Credibility gap? The language we teach and the language we use

Della Summers, *Longman Dictionaries*

This title is intended to be challenging, to throw down the gauntlet to language teachers and authors of coursebooks and grammars, to convince them that the advent of corpora, particularly spoken corpora, should change EFL books dramatically.

Longman has collected two spoken corpora:

- the 10-million-word spoken corpus that is part of the British National Corpus, which was created by a consortium including OUP, Chambers, Lancaster University and OUCS;
- a new 5-million-word corpus of American spoken English gathered in the USA.

Both corpuses are designed to give a true picture of spoken English for both Britain and the US by recording a valid cross-section of the populations. Together they represent around 3000 hours of talking – about one year's talk by one individual if you think of eight hours being the number of hours in a day when someone could be speaking, i.e. when they are not asleep or doing other silent things!

Context and speaker relationship

The thing that leaps out at you as you study authentic material is the overwhelming importance of the *context* in which the conversation happens and the *relationship* between the speakers in conversations.

Consider the difference of the language learning context of the EFL learner and the native-speaker learner of English. As a child, you learn over a long period a few words at a time; you can learn at a pace that suits you; your teacher is endlessly patient – delighted at every new word you produce. You don't need to know that *chair* is a noun and *sit* is a verb. Even if you make a 'grammatical' mistake like saying *I wented to the shops* instead of *I went to the shops*, this could well be greeted by a round of applause rather than a sigh of exasperation. You have very little pressure – no classmates to keep up with and no exam to pass, and you are surrounded by helpful input to enable you understand what is going on. You learn in context, through doing things, on a one-to-one basis.

Everything is so much more difficult for EFL learners. They learn in a classroom environment. Much of the language studied is written English. In many countries learning is still dominated by translation from English to the native language. The tapes or videos used are usually specially scripted so that the 'context' is created in a vacuum by an author or team of authors. There is no naturally occurring situation which gives rise to the language, and equally important, no social relationship to underpin the language. So it's no wonder that some coursebook conversations sound a trifle artificial.

The corpuses now available have already dramatically changed dictionaries for EFL students, as the *Cobuild* and other dictionaries show. But we have yet to see the revolution impacting very much on coursebooks.

Real spoken language

This is a conversation from the British National Corpus between two 15-year-old girls from the Midlands, discussing one of their school friends who has brought a birthday cake to school and a television programme called *Inspector Morse*.

Emma: No, I don't hate her, she just annoys me badly!

Kelly: That's all!

Emma: She made [erm] ... Heather a birthday cake the other day and, I, I've got to say actually this cake was pretty good, but like she had to take it to school! I mean, the girl is sad! If you're gonna take a birthday cake to school, I mean, that is sad, isn't it?

Kelly: My brain's just died!

Emma: But that is very very sad! But like er, she took it to school, and Scott was giving us a lift to school so she didn't have to walk and she's in the car and she's going if this gets, if this gets all smashed up, Scott, I hope you realise I'm blaming you! And she was serious! I was thinking

Kelly: I would've turned round and told her to get out.

Emma: I did.

Kelly: Get out the car! [laugh]

Emma: I said, I just went, I just said to her look, Hannah, you don't have to come in the car! And like, I said it jokingly but with

Kelly: Mm

Emma: With that sort of hint

Kelly: With that sort of with that sort of I'm dying to stick this knife [laughing] in your back!

Emma: Yeah.

Kelly: Oh!

Emma: Oh, did you see Inspector Morse last night?
Kelly: No, I saw the very end bit.
Emma: Did you see the ... where's she ... where that girl stabbed er ... her ... What was that girl in? I was sat there, me and my dad were going, what has she been in?
Kelly: She was in [erm]
Emma: Got a really irritating voice, hasn't she?
Kelly: You know where there was that ... there was the young girl ... and there was the old wo ... oldish woman who was supposed to be a film star or something?
Emma: Oh yeah! That thing where [erm]... she, she worked for him, didn't she?
Kelly: Yeah.
Emma: She lived in that hotel.
Kelly: Mm.
Emma: Oh yes, I remember... Oh that thing that was supposed to be funny.
Kelly: It was crap, wasn't it!

The function of fillers such as *like* and *I mean* is to give the speaker time for mental processing, to think of exactly the right word or how to say exactly what they want to say, with just the effect that they want. This usage is documented in corpus-based ELT dictionaries like the *Longman Dictionary of Contemporary English* with this example:

*This bloke will look at it for me, **like**, and he'll tell me what it needs.*

The usage is marked SPOKEN, but including it in a large advanced level dictionary does make information about this use of this word available to any student or teacher who has occasion to look it up. It does not recommend students to use it themselves. If some teachers disapprove of usages such as *like*, they should be aware that this usage is not confined to less educated speakers of English. We all do it, including the most refined and correct speakers of English.

The lexis of spoken English

Sad is a vogue word particularly common in teen language at the moment, meaning 'not cool'. *Badly* in Emma's opening utterance means 'a lot'. A 15-year-old could say, *She likes him **badly*** or even *She likes him well **badly***. Here *badly* is not negative; it is an intensifier taking its meaning from the clause or adverbial phrase it modifies. This usage is restricted to one group of speakers – young people – so we do not record them even in an advanced ELT dictionary like the *LDCE*, but *sad* is entered, with this example from the spoken corpus:

***sad** /sæd/ adj ...* **5** *... I think Carol's a bit of a sad name. Oh sorry, is your Mum's name Carol?*

Sad in this sense is common enough for students who listen to pop music or watch films like *Trainspotting* to hear it and want to know what it means – but do they need to know it well enough to use it themselves?

The grammar of spoken English

Questions

There are a lot of questions, and especially question tags in Emma and Kelly's conversation. In fact questions in general are much more frequent in spoken material than in written material. They are used not only to ask direct questions, like *Where do you live?* but also to check that your conversation partner is still listening and is not in disagreement.

Tag questions are much more frequent in British speech than American speech, perhaps because the British are more tentative and less confident than the Americans, so instead of saying *We should go now*, the British might say *We should make a move now, shouldn't we?* or something else equally indirect.

So is spoken grammar quite different from written grammar? Do Emma and Kelly use the same parts of speech as we find in written English? Does every utterance have a subject and an object where we would expect to find them in written English? Does the word order change dramatically?

There is much about the grammar of spoken English that is the same as in written English, but there are important differences too.

In *Got a really irritating voice, hasn't she?* we see the typical omission of words in spoken English, which you only get in written English when it mimics spoken English. Exactly who the 'she' is is transparent in context; it is implicit, so it can be missed out. This is something special about spoken English – it is very economical. If a word can be missed out, it usually will be missed out, because the person you are talking to can ask you who you mean if necessary. For example,

A: *Do you want to watch TV?*
B: ^ *Might.* (Subject omitted)
^ *You serious?* (Verb omitted)

This is the way speech works. We teach contractions like *I couldn't find it* and *She won't be coming*, but only a few coursebooks teach omission of words in this way.

Social/interpersonal function of speech

Conversation often has a primarily social or interpersonal function, compared with the more informative function of much writing. Even the use of tag questions in the transcript is not really intended to check that Kelly understands or agrees about the facts, but rather that she supports Emma's opinions, which are given freely throughout the conversation and are largely critical or negative. The point is to prove solidarity in that they both watch the same TV programmes, that they have the same likes and dislikes, and share the same social context.

By comparison, written English is expository, with explanation or the giving of information as its primary function. That is why it is written down. Written English sentences are longer than spoken sentences – if they can be called sentences (the notion of a sentence with a full stop at the end and a capital letter at the beginning being essentially an abstraction, a way of making language definite rather than vague). Writing is our way of making language explicit rather than implicit.

Strong language in spoken English

The tape shows the strong tendency in speech towards hyperbole – strong language used for effect. We say *I'm starving*, rather than *I'm hungry; he's gorgeous*, rather than *he's nice-looking*. This feature becomes apparent when studying very large amounts of authentic data such as our spoken corpora. For example, Kelly says

My brain's just died (meaning I can't cope with how boring it is to take a birthday cake to school)

AND

with that sort of I'm dying to stick this knife in your back (meaning I'm sick of you).

These strong reactions to the story about the cake are all turned outwards; they are about people who are not there. In fact, an important purpose of conversation is to give opinions or build joint opinions with the person you are talking to. It reinforces the social bond between the girls.

Should students be presented with this information? Is this linguistic imperialism, where we foist our own particular cultural tendencies on students who want to be able to communicate mainly in writing, probably in order to speak to other non-native speakers of English, who have their own variety of spoken English as well?

Politeness in spoken English

The opposite side of this is the tendency towards politeness between speakers in the same conversation. Their aggression is directed outwards from their conversation, outwards from their relationship. Between themselves they tend to be polite.

This point is substantiated by a three-year corpus analysis project led by Doug Biber of the University of Northern Arizona, an authority on computational analysis of text and corpora, working on a new corpus-based grammar of English with Geoffrey Leech of Lancaster University, Stig Johansson of Oslo University, and Ed Finnegan of Columbia University. Finnegan points out in the forthcoming *Longman Grammar of Spoken and Written English*

> There is a marked tendency in conversation to agree to requests or offers. Politeness dictates that acceptance is the norm, so the expression of acceptance may be comparatively brief, whereas a refusal, not being the norm, is usually accompanied by an explanation or comment.

Agreement is often monosyllabic:

A: Do you want some milk?
B: Mm.

Examples of disagreement, or turning down an offer, usually need an explanation:

A: Can I see the picture?
B: Well, I'm reading the article.

A: Can I get you some more soup?
B: No. I'm fine. I'm saving the room.

In the *Longman Essential Activator*, a production dictionary for intermediate students, the pragmatics of spoken English is covered in the *Essential Communication* pages designed to help students express themselves naturally in speech. In the page on 'Suggestions', students are shown how to reply *yes* to suggestions and that if you reply *no*, you normally have to give a reason to justify the refusal, otherwise you may be taken as rude or unfriendly.

Ensuring understanding

This is one of the prime requirements of conversation, so in the sentence

I just gave it away, didn't I, Rudy, my knitting?

it is not crystal clear what 'it' refers to, so the speaker clarified with a trailer at the end of the sentence to make it clear that 'it' refers to her knitting.

It is both speakers' job to make sure that understanding has been accomplished, or in terms of the work on relevance theory by Sperber and Wilson, that relevance has been accomplished – in other words that you have said what you wanted to, your hearer has understood what you wanted, and that it has all been done in the shortest and most economical way.

Implicitness/cultural knowledge
Being economical in speech often relies very heavily on shared knowledge. The participants in a conversation share not only physical time and space, they also share a common set of knowledge. So to take an example from the Longman American Spoken Corpus, when someone says *Have you seen Susan's baby yet?*, they both know which Susan out of all the potential thousands of Susans is referred to. Or take the following extract from the British National Corpus:

A: I forgot that ... I discovered that all our letters now are apt to be a day late. I didn't know until the other day.
B: What because
A: Because they come through Aldershot and they all have to go through the scanner.

Both speakers know why mail that comes through Aldershot would be scanned, because they know that the British Army headquarters is in Aldershot, and mail might be scanned because of the possibility of letter bombs. There is no explanation for this in the conversation – it is implicitly understood. This makes it difficult to take examples direct from the corpus, as with this corpus-based entry for *intimate*

He surprised me with his ***intimate*** *knowledge of Kierkegaard and Schopenhauer*

The meaning of *intimate* would be lost on many students, because it relies on the reader understanding who Kierkegaard and Schopenhauer are. If they don't know that they are 19th-century philosophers famous for being difficult to understand, the students will not get the point of why anyone should be surprised that someone should have intimate knowledge of them.

Decontextualised sentences
Coursebooks (and grammars) are full of decontextualised single sentences, written as though they were speech, as in this unit on 'Going to'

If I were you I wouldn't go to England for your summer holiday – it'll probably rain.
You wait and see – she'll leave college, and then she'll get married and have a baby.
Something tells me we're going to have sausages for lunch.
Let's get out of here. There's going to be trouble.

The reason these decontextualised sentences seem unnatural is not just because they rely heavily on stereotypes. They offend against the rules of implicitness and explicitness described above. They seem to be real sentences, but there is no before and no after, no cohesion, and they are therefore unconvincing.

Real corpus examples taken out of context can suffer from similar problems, as in this corpus-based dictionary example:

'But Jesus is here!' the priest intoned.

The context is missing, and that makes this sentence on its own faintly ludicrous.

References to people's names and to place-names in example sentences can be confusing too, as in this corpus-based grammar book example

As usual, I was woken up by Ark licking my face.

Who or what is 'Ark', we ask ourselves.

There is a middle way, which avoids overdependence on context, while preserving the life and reality of the language that the corpus can present to us. Here are some example sentences from the *Longman Essential Activator*, a production dictionary where it is of paramount importance that the examples clarify, as their function is to be model sentences for intermediate students. The *Essential Activator* is organized around 600 basic words or ideas, like *easy*, *about*, *enjoy* and *material*. The student is guided towards other vocabulary items to express those ideas more appropriately.

EASY
it's easy *"How do you print out files from your disk?" "It's easy. You just click on the Print icon".*

ABOUT (= approximately)
give or take *She's been working here for 2 years, give or take a few weeks.*

ENJOY
good fun *Have you ever been windsurfing? It's really good fun.*

MATERIAL
stuff *Do you have any of that clear plastic stuff for covering food with?*

Each of these entries is also marked with a speech bubble to indicate that it is 'typical of speech'.

These are examples that are corpus-based, but not corpus-bound. Perhaps coursebooks could gain some benefits, in the same way that ELT dictionaries have, by being based, in part, on the natural language of spoken corpora.

5.6 Exploiting task recordings for the grammar of spoken English

Jane Willis, *Aston University*

We looked first at the nature of spontaneous speech and the reasons why its grammar differs from that of planned or written language. Then, examining transcripts of spoken data, we identified typical grammatical features to look out for.

Spontaneous speech is interactive, dynamic and (usually) cooperative, so there are various linguistic devices that participants use to sustain the interaction and aid turn-taking. For example, **interactive markers:** *you know*; **use of tags:** *isn't it?, mm?*; **evaluative phrases:** *Mm, Yeah, That's amazing, That's funny actually, because ...*

Since we are composing in real-time and simply don't have time to plan what we want to say word by word, we use a lot of short, often pre-fabricated, chunks. **Ellipsis** is common – we omit verbs or subject words and often do without inversion or modals in questions: *Not far away/No very near, But you get the main line in?, Trying to get fit.*

Vagueness is acceptable, and phrases like *or something like that* are typical.

We often bring the vital part of the message forward for emphasis, resulting in different word order: *It's Hatton Garden I work, Car numbers I can never remember.* (This is similar to word order in Japanese, where the new comes first.)

We signal topic shifts and closings: *Another thing is ..., So that was it really.*

We report – twice as often in speech as in writing – what other people think or tell us: *He was saying, She thought he'd ...*

Nominal groups are far simpler in speech, and we tend to link narrative with *and* and *and then* rather than use verb structures with *-ing* or *-ed* such as *Excited by the noise, they ...*

Learners of English are generally more familiar with written text, and the grammar they learn is written grammar. They often attempt to speak written English – difficult for fluent speakers to do in real-time! If learners want to speak spontaneously, and understand real-time conversation, then it is vital they are given opportunities to hear and study it.

We found that by asking fluent speakers of English to record a range of communication tasks, (tasks that students will actually perform in class), and then transcribing selectively, we could use the recordings and transcriptions in class (after students had done the task themselves) for listening practice and material for language study. A study carried out by Wilson (1994) revealed that such recordings illustrated almost all features of spontaneous interactive English, the only marked lack being (not surprisingly) examples of topic shift.

Using transcripts of tasks about a *Cat's Feat*, I illustrated three starting points for language analysis or consciousness-raising activities:

- semantic concepts – themes, notions, functions – e.g. phrases of location
- a particular word (e.g. *it*), highlighting its various uses and patterns
- categories of meaning or use.

We also discussed lexical chunks. I gave some tips for making task recordings, underlining the need for publishers to provide books with authentic, unedited interaction (not just interview talk).

5.7 Textbook dialogues and conversation analysis

Susan Mandala, *University of Cambridge*

While ELT textbooks have improved substantially in the past 30–40 years in terms of overall pedagogical value, the dialogues in these textbooks do not seem to have changed significantly despite shifts in teaching priorities and methods. A comparison of language teaching dialogues published recently with those published 250 years ago indicates that they are a remarkably conservative form, exhibiting only superficial changes in lexis and topic over time.

Research comparing textbook language and natural talk reveals that textbooks are often inaccurate in their portrayal of native speaker speech. They have been criticised for presenting the written standard rather than the spoken norm, and for modelling speech act functions rarely used in natural speech. Similarly, textbook dialogues have been found to present an unbalanced, simplistic view of talk which does not faithfully depict the complexity of natural speech events. It is claimed that this deficiency may mislead students as to what is considered pragmatically appropriate in English conversation.

Based on these findings, it is typically recommended that analyses of natural, native speaker interaction inform the development of textbook dialogues. The tools for this procedure currently exist: various corpora of native speaker talk have been collected, and conversational processes such as turn-taking and topic management are well understood. But the question still remains how to go from corpus to coursebook. It is suggested here that conversation analysis can be used to evaluate dialogues *as talk*, and that findings from these evaluations can be used to modify textbook dialogues, bringing them more into line with natural talk norms without sacrificing their pedagogical usefulness. Thus, what is needed in order to fully exploit corpora as resources in materials development is not only a complete analysis of natural speech, but also a complete analysis of textbook dialogues.

A preliminary investigation was conducted exploring the move structure of advice-giving encounters in textbook dialogues and natural talk. As with previous research, it was discovered that the textbook dialogues generally lacked evaluative follow-up moves. While it is tempting at this point to offer the addition of follow-up moves as a solution, this may be premature. A more in-depth comparison between natural talk and textbook dialogues reveals that for advice-giving, the placement of the follow-up move, and not only its frequency, is the crucial factor. While dialogues tend to present several advising exchanges, each offering a different piece of advice, the natural talk encounters tend to develop one piece of advice throughout the talk. It was generally after this one piece of advice had been delivered that the follow-up move was used to shut down the encounter.

5.8 Plenary: How can text analysis help us teach reading?

Michael Hoey, *University of Liverpool*

There are three features of text which are pivotal to any attempt to answer the question posed in my title, and none of them is particularly controversial. Most text-linguists agree that text is interactive, patterned and cohesive.

In this paper I shall suggest that each of these features can play a central role in developing reading strategies that will help the learner access authentic data that would otherwise be well beyond his or her reading capabilities. The data I shall use is an article entitled 'Quietly Vanishing' by Malcolm Smith, published in the *Independent on Sunday* in the *Sunday Review* section on 23 March 1997. I chose this text because it is long enough (73 sentences) to give me the opportunity to make the points I wish to make, short enough (one complete page in the original) to be manageable as an appendix, timeless enough in its content (the decline of the dormouse in England and Wales) to make it seem worth the effort of analysis, and – most crucially – it appeared the day before I was due to send the organisers of IATEFL my handout requirements. It was not chosen because after painstaking investigation it was found to support my arguments; it was irrevocably chosen before analysis on it could commence. As a self-standing scientific article of 73 sentences' length, it is clearly both too long and too complicated for anyone without near-native mastery of the language (or a lot of patience).

1 Text is interactive

Text is the product of a writer's attempts to answer a reader's anticipated questions; the readers, for their part, have to work out what questions a writer is attempting to answer (Widdowson, 1979; Winter, 1977; Gray, 1977; Hoey, 1979). Just because they do this instinctively in their L1 does not mean that they will do so without prompting in their L2. If the learners come from a culture with significant genre differences, their predictions may in any case be markedly different from those a native speaker would make (cf. Kaplan, 1966, 1977; Houghton & Hoey, 1983; Connor, 1987; Purves [ed.] 1988).

Sometimes, though, a writer feels the need to spell out for us the questions he or she is answering and when this happens it is usually because those questions are central to the writer's message. Questions can be spelt out either by means of a rhetorical question or by the use of embedded questions (as in the ancient beer slogan *What we want is Watney's*. More subtly, writers can use a special vocabulary that refers to the questions a text is answering, e.g. *question, answer, explanation*. A sentence such as *The **explanation** was simple* tells us to expect an answer to a question that may have only up to this point been implicit in the preceding text.

Since the presence of these markers is evidence that the writer has certain questions in mind, it follows that they are clues to the reader about the key points and potential drift of the paper they occur in. Try looking for them in the dormouse article in the Appendix. You should find that sentences 2, 13, 20, 23, 28, 65 and 66 all have one or more such markers. Try reading them together, picking up pronoun referents from preceding sentences where necessary. You will find that they make a surprising amount of sense – surprising, that is, until one remembers that what one is picking up on is the writer's own signals to us about what he thinks is important in his text.

2 Text is patterned

That text is patterned is generally agreed by text linguists, though some would refer to generic structures, some to schemata and some (like myself) to culturally popular patterns. Each approach has its strengths, depending on what one is trying to achieve. Here I am going to refer to 'culturally popular patterns', which might be thought of as configurations of questions that readers and writers agree to expect. They can be represented diagrammatically as follows:

If we see these text patterns as configurations of questions that writer and reader expect to be answered, we might expect these too to be signalled as important by writers – and indeed they are. Winter (1977) drew attention to a large vocabulary whose specialist function was to signal to readers the pattern being used. Words such as *problem*, *difficulty* and *need*, or *solution*, *do about* and *answer* are signposts from the writer to the reader to follow him or her up well-trodden paths. (Winter, 1977; Hoey, 1979, 1983; Jordan, 1984).

In long texts, such as the dormouse text, there are often several patterns co-existent in the text. In this text, for example, there is both a *Problem – Response* pattern and a *Gap in Knowledge – Filling* pattern. Hints of both are in fact present in the subtitle to the text, which talks of studies and what they have revealed (both

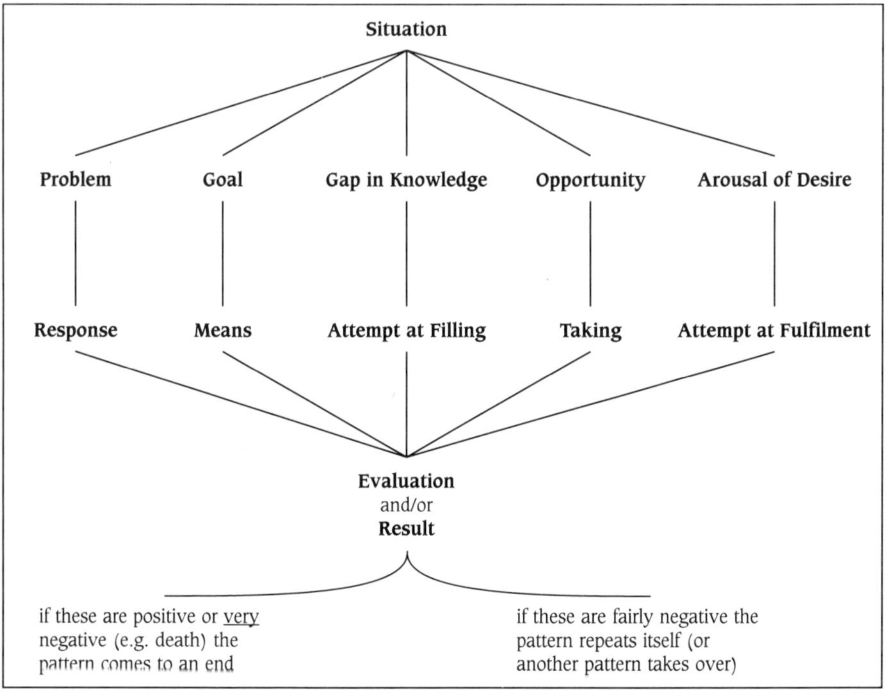

markers of a *Gap in Knowledge – Filling* pattern) and of disappearance (which implies a *Problem* for the poor dormouse). If we then chase up those sentences in the main text that contain further signals of the *Gap in Knowledge* pattern, we find that signals occur in sentences 2 (*studies*), 13 (*shed some light*), 20 (*results, show*), 23 (*survey, clarifies*), 28 (*understanding why*) and 69 (*research*). Try reading those sentences together and you will find they make good sense, despite their comprising only 10% of the text. To be able to select these sentences, the learner needs to be able to recognise the special vocabulary, but does not have to attempt to make sense of the text until he or she has found the relevant sentences. Nor is there any vicious circle here: identification of the common vocabulary involved is all that is required of the learner; the pay-off is a readable abridgement of the text, one that, as regards length, a reader could hope to cope with.

A similar point might be made about the *Problem – Response* pattern in the text. If you collect together those sentences that contain one of the common signals of *Problem*, you get sentences 29 (*requirements*), 35 (*problem*), 38 (*needs*), 41 (*unable, lack, restriction*), 42 (*needs*), 45 (*has to*), 47 (*need*), 55 (*unsuitable*), 59 (*drawback*) and 61 (*vulnerable, poor*). Most of these signals are very common items in the language, largely because the pattern itself is so common. If you read these sentences together, ignoring conjuncts like *however* and *so* which are not meaningful out of their original context, you will find that, as before, the selection makes sense.

The same is true if you identify the sentences that contain signals of *Response*. What I have been suggesting is that the learner can hunt out the signals laid down by the writer and identify the sentences that contain them. Since these signals are mostly common and useful words in the language, the search itself is a worthwhile vocabulary-learning exercise. Having identified the sentences with the requisite signals, the learner then reads them to get a shaped sense of what the text is all about. Neither method is without its defects, however. In the first place, the learner has to be able to recognise the relevant vocabularies. Secondly, not every text is so signalled (the hit rate is good, though).

The third technique I want to briefly sketch has the virtue of being less dependent on the signalling style of the writer.

3 Text is cohesive

The most widely recognised feature of text is that it is cohesive (Halliday & Hasan, 1976). Cohesion is (with the exception of conjuncts) largely a side-product of our need to repeat when we write. We cannot say everything we want to in one sentence, so we are forced to break our message up into manageable chunks and to connect the chunks and show how the chunks relate by using repetition. One important feature of this necessity is that sentences that share an above average amount of common (repeated) material have a strong tendency to make sense together, even if they are some way apart (Hoey, 1991). Consider for example the following two sentences from the dormouse text:

(13) Both [studies] are by Dr Paul Bright and Dr Pat Morris of Royal Holloway, University of London – with the collaboration of Dr Tony Mitchell-Jones of

English Nature on the distribution survey – and manage finally to shed some light on why the dormouse is so rare.

(60) According to Bright and Morris, the best sites support up to eight dormice per hectare, compared, for example, with a minimum of 130 bank voles.

There is repetition of *Bright*, *Morris* and *dormouse/dormice* and the pair of sentences make good sense, despite being separated by 46 sentences. This is quite normal and is found to be the case in over 90% of pairs connected by three or more repetitions. It is also equally true of other texts. Nor is it the case that the phenomenon operates this way because it is so rare. In most texts of the type we are considering there are many such pairs. To give you an idea of just how many, the following list shows all the sentences that the first thirteen sentences in the text share three or more repetitions with:

All of this may be of interest but it may not be obvious how it is relevant to the needs of the language learner. After all, the average language learner is not going to analyse the patterns of repetition in a long text, the analytical work of many hours, in order to find pairs of sentences that make sense together. Fortunately, a practical reading strategy can be developed from this curious fact about text without turning the learner into a text linguist! Quite simply, the learner needs to take an early sentence with some meat on it – in this case the subtitle looks to be a good candidate – and make sure he or she fully understands it, looking up any unfamiliar words as necessary. Then he or she looks for another sentence in the text that repeats three lexical items from it, repetition here being as broad or as narrow as the learner can cope with; the advanced learner will look for synonyms and pronoun repetitions, while the less

Sentence	**Shares three or more repetitions with sentence/s**	
1	7, 11, 12, 13, 20, 21 (arguably), 24, 27	coherent with all of them
2	23	coherent with it
3, 4, 5	none	
6	14	coherent with it
7	1, 11 (arguably), 12, 13, 53	coherent with all bar 53
8	none	
9	29, 61, 69	coherent with all of them
10	64	coherent with it
11	1, 7 (arguably)	coherent with both of them
12	1, 7, 13, 30, 69	coherent with all bar 30
13	1, 7, 12, 14, 23, 24, 30, 34, 60	coherent with all bar 30; partially coherent with 24

advanced will focus on exact or near exact repetitions only. Since almost all pairs make sense, it does not much matter which approach is adopted, though obviously there are more sentences connected by repetition that is not exact than connected only by exact repetition. When the learner finds a sentence which repeats three of the items from his or her earlier sentence, he or she reads it – simple as that! And it should make sense, unless he or she is unlucky or unless he or she has wrongly identified something as repeating when it is not (e.g. *appear* in sentence 7 does not repeat *disappeared* in sentence 1, despite the shared stem). Having got sense from the second sentence, the learner then continues to search and to read anything he or she comes across that meets the criterion. In this way he or she will make sense of a far from random selection set of sentences that will give a flavour of the original, encourage the development of useful vocabulary, and make him or her feel they are really getting something out of their learning.

Try it for yourself. Look, for example, at the sentences that connect with the 13 sentences in the list above. Try reading all the sentences that connect with sentence 1 or sentence 7; you will be surprised how coherent they are (subject, as always, to the removal of conjuncts like *so* and the supplying of referents for pronouns).

Perhaps the main lesson to be learnt from looking at text analysis is not that this technique or that technique can be applied, but that texts are networks of information and it really is not necessary to read everything to get a great deal of sense out of that network. Every text is a miniature hypertext, a tiny web, and repetitions, lexical signals and makers of questions are all routes through the web, choice-points within the hypertext. If we can encourage our learners to see texts as resources of meaning rather than monoliths to be taken as a whole or not at all, we will be encouraging them to read in a way that puts them in charge and enables them to tackle texts that are intellectually at their level but which would previously have been thought too hard. If text analysis helps you to help them to get to this happy position, I will be more than happy.

References

Connor, Ulla (1987) Argumentative patterns in student essays: Cross-cultural differences. In Connor U & R B Kaplan (Eds) *Writing Across Languages: Analysis of L2 Text Reading* MA: Addison-Wesley 57–71

Gray, Bennison (1977) From discourse to dialog *Journal of Pragmatics* 1.3 283–98

Halliday, M A K & Ruqaiya Hasan (1976) *Cohesion in English* London: Longman

Hoey, Michael (1979) *Signalling in Discourse* Discourse Analysis Monographs No 6 Birmingham: English Language Research, University of Birmingham (Abridged as Signalling in discourse: a functional analysis of a common discourse pattern in written and spoken English. In Malcolm Coulthard (Ed.) 1994 *Advances in Written Text Analysis* London: Routledge 1994 26–45)

Hoey, Michael (1983) *On the Surface of Discourse* London: George Allen & Unwin (Reprinted 1991 Nottingham: Department of English Studies, University of Nottingham)

Hoey, Michael (1991) *Patterns of Lexis in Text* Oxford: Oxford University Press

Houghton, Diane & Michael Hoey (1983) Linguistics and written discourse: Contrastive rhetorics. In Kaplan R B, R L Jones & G R Tucker (Eds.) *Annual Review of Applied Linguistics* III Rowley, MA: Newbury House 2–22

Jordan, Michael P (1984) *Rhetoric of Everyday English Texts* London: George Allen & Unwin

Kaplan, Robert B (1966) Cultural thought patterns in inter-cultural education *Language Learning* 1–20

Kaplan, Robert B (1977) Contrastive rhetoric: some hypotheses *ITL* 39/40, 61–72

Purves, Alan C (Ed.) (1988) *Writing Across Languages and Cultures: Issues in Contrastive Rhetoric* (Written Communication Annual, Vol 2) Newbury Park: Sage Publications

Widdowson, Henry (1979) *Explorations in Applied Linguistics* Oxford: Oxford University Press

Winter, Eugene O (1977) A clause relational approach to English texts: a study of some predictive lexical items *Instructional Science* 6.1 1–91

Appendix

QUIETLY VANISHING

(1) Two new studies of the elusive dormouse have revealed that it has disappeared from several counties in England. (2) Malcolm Smith reports on why its geographical range is shrinking.

(3) Lewis Carroll could not have been more accurate. (4) In *Alice's Adventures in Wonderland* he wrote: (4.1) 'There was a table set out under a tree in front of the house, and the March Hare and the Hatter were having tea at it. (4.2) A dormouse was sitting between them, fast asleep, and the other two were using it as a cushion, resting their elbows on it, and talking over its head. (4.3) "Very uncomfortable for the dormouse," thought Alice, "only as it's asleep, I suppose it doesn't mind".'

(5) This picture of a languorous dormouse, snoozing its time away and looked down on by everyone around it, sums up the life of one of our most engaging little mammals. (6) Attractive, with its golden brown fur and long, bushy tail and well known from stories such as Carroll's, it is nonetheless rarely seen and understood. (7) Only two scientific studies appear to have been published about British dormice this century.

(8) Unfortunate though it is, the dormouse is one of nature's ready-made victims. (9) It has exacting ecological requirements which make it vulnerable, particularly to habitat change, as well as to climatic variation. (10) It lives at a low population density and has a very low rate of population increase. (11) And because it hibernates for half of the year (from October to at least April, depending upon the weather) and is mainly nocturnal, it is not an easy creature to study.

(12) Nevertheless, two studies, one on the distribution of the dormouse, the other about its ecological needs, have been published recently. (13) Both are by Dr Paul Bright and Dr Pat Morris of Royal Holloway, University of London – with the collaboration of Dr Tony Mitchell-Jones of English Nature on the distribution survey – and manage finally to shed some light on why the dormouse is so rare.

(14) To plot the distribution of the dormouse, it is no use relying on sighting these six-inch long (from nose to tip of tail) squirrel-like mice. (15) The more productive way is to search for opened hazelnuts in woodland. (16) Dormouse gnawed nuts have a different pattern of marks from those opened [by] other creatures. (17) As a result, the Great Nut Hunt was launched in 1993, with the help of the Countryside Council for Wales and English Nature, and attracted no

less than 6,500 participants (people, not dormice). (18) Out of more than 172,000 gnawed nuts, 1,352 were confirmed as dormouse-nibbled, identifying 334 dormouse sites in England and Wales. (19) They have never been known to occur in Scotland.

(20) What the results of the Great Nut Hunt show is how confined to southern Britain this mammal now is. (21) A quarter of its known sites are in Devon and 12 per cent in Dorset, the two counties in which the dormouse is most abundant. (22) Other southern English counties have a scattering, as do the Welsh borders and a few woods in the north, west and south of Wales.

(23) The survey clarifies the extent to which the dormouse's range has contracted. (24) According to the naturalist and illustrator, Archibald Thorburn, writing in 1920, the dormouse was 'fairly plentiful in the southern and western counties of England, though rare in the Midlands and Norfolk'. (25) It was, he wrote, abundant in parts of Surrey. (26) Not now. (27) It is seemingly extinct in several counties where it was found late last century. (28) Understanding why is the key to trying to hold on to the populations that remain and, maybe, even help them expand.

(29) First, we need to look at its habitat requirements. (30) The three plant species most associated with dormice – hazel, honeysuckle and bramble – are widely distributed throughout Britain in woods, copses and hedgerows. (31) Hazelnuts are the main fattening-up food consumed prior to hibernation. (32) Honeysuckle offers flowers in springtime, with fruits later in the summer, and finely shredded bark which is the favoured nesting material. (33) Bramble is valuable for its late summer and early autumn fruit supply.

(34) 'None of these three species is absolutely vital,' argue Bright and Morris, 'provided suitable substitutes exist, but few very good dormouse sites are without more than one of them.' (35) The problem is that in many woods managed primarily for timber, hazel can take up unproductive space while bramble is a nuisance and climbing plants such as honeysuckle are sometimes cut down. (36) In woods grazed by sheep – common in Wales and the north of England – such shrubs struggle to survive.

(37) The structure of a good dormouse wood is important. (38) It needs to have a well-grown, unshaded understorey of shrubs and small trees so that the sunlight encourages plenty of flowers and fruits. (39) Dense woodlands, or planted rows of trees, are anathema for such frugivorous fantasies. (40) Equally important is a variety of shrubs; a wide range of flowering and fruiting times is more likely to offer a suitable menu. (41) Dormice are unable to digest cellulose-rich foods easily, such as leaves, because they lack a large intestine, yet another restriction. (42) Furthermore, the shrub- and small-tree-rich understorey needs to be physically continuous so that dormice can move in the dark from branch to branch without having to touch the ground. (43) Simple really.

(44) For nesting, they often use tree holes and hollows, but sometimes they take over old squirrels['] dreys or birds' nests. (45) So, an understorey-rich wood, with not too many larger, shade-bearing trees still has to possess older trees because these are most likely to have natural holes.

(46) The hibernation spot is different again – a cool place on the ground, often in a rock crevice, tree stump or rodent burrow. (47) Surprisingly, for such fussy fellows, dormice take avidly to nest boxes which can mimic the tree holes they need for summer nests. (48) In woods short of natural holes, but endowed with the structure and variety of shrubs required, putting up nest boxes could bolster flagging populations.

(49) But, back to the limitations. (50) Dormice don't move over long distances, but exploit food supplies in perhaps one hectare of woodland over a year, harvesting different spots and shrubs as the seasons change. (51) In one night, radio tracking has shown that they may travel between 150 and 300 metres, but no more than 70 metres in a straight line from the nest, relying on the local knowledge they build up of

which shrubs have food and which branches interconnect.

(52) Little wonder, then, that woodland loss and the fragmentation of what native woodland remains have reduced substantially the number of dormouse-suitable habitats. (53) A couple of thousand years ago the bulk of lowland Britain was wooded and one can only assume that dormice were much more commonplace.

(54) Today, remnants of this ancient wildwood cover no more than a small percentage of land. (55) Recent plantations of conifers or broad-leaved trees are usually unsuitable for the dormouse which hasn't adapted to the changes we have wrought. (56) The one exception is that they have moved into some hedgerows, especially older ones with a variety of fruiting shrubs and a dense structure. (57) But hedgerows are in decline too; 150,000 kilometres have been lost since 1945. (58) Hedgerows are also often the only physical link between one isolated wood and the next.

(59) Apart from habitat, its other major drawback is the dormouse's population dynamics. (60) According to Bright and Morris, the best sites support up to eight dormice per hectare, compared, for example, with a minimum of 130 bank voles. (61) So small woods have few dormice, making them highly vulnerable if, for instance, woodland management is altered or there is a succession of poor summers for fruit supply. (62) As only one or two youngsters per female are successfully reared each year, the population rises slowly. (63) Perhaps to compensate, dormice can live up to five years – much longer than, say, bank voles, half of which die before they reach four months.

(64) Relatively untouched by predators – probably because they spend their lives in branches and bushes – the dormouse's lifestyle strategy of a long life, low production of youngsters and low population densities is fine in large areas of suitable habitat under stable conditions. (65) But it is the opposite of what it needs to succeed in today's sparse woods, many of which don't provide the structure and menu these fussy animals need.

(66) One thing it does get right is its lengthy hibernation – a strategy which overcomes winter food shortages. (67) But, ironically, mild winters are probably more of a threat than cold ones, simply because its fat reserves are depleted faster as its metabolic rate rises. (68) Long, mild British winters, albeit with cold spells, may not be in its favour.

(69) More research on the ecology of dormice is going to be necessary. (70) In the meantime, this mammal is starting to get the attention it deserves, courtesy of an action plan agreed by the government and its conservation agencies. (71) The objectives are to maintain and enhance existing populations, improve woodland management to encourage them, and reintroduce them to suitable woods in at least five counties in which they have been lost.

(72) No longer is the dormouse being ignored. (73) Alice would be ever so pleased.

('Quietly Vanishing' by Malcolm Smith in *The Sunday Review,* ***Independent on Sunday*** 23 March 1997, page 50)

5.9 Teaching intonation for English as an international language: Teachability, learnability and intelligibility

Jennifer Jenkins, *King's College, London*

I began by making two points about pronunciation in general: we cannot assume that what is real (done by native speakers) is either realistic for teaching and learning, or relevant for international uses of English, in the sense of contributing to intelligibility in contexts where all speakers are non-native speakers of English.

The issue of teachability and learnability was then examined. Support was given to the suggestion of Dalton and Seidlhofer that we regard these as being on a scale, with some aspects of pronunciation being 'fairly easy to describe and to generalise' and thus 'teachable' but others being 'extremely dependent on individual circumstances and therefore nearly impossible to isolate out for direct teaching', and so 'better left for learning without teacher intervention' (*Pronunciation in the Scheme for Teacher Education* OUP 1994 72–73).

One area of intonation widely thought to be unteachable is pitch movement to express attitude, the so-called 'attitudinal function' of intonation. However, I argued that lack of teachability applies not merely to the expression of attitudes, but to pitch movement in general. In support of my claim, I drew attention to the following:

- grammar and pitch movement do not go hand in hand – 'There is no melody which is exclusively associated with one type of sentence' (Kreidler C *The Pronunciation of English* Blackwell 1989 182–3);
- Brazil's theory of Discourse Intonation may reflect what native speakers actually do, but the given-new dichotomy is ambiguous. Determining what is new and what is given information involves many factors, making the dichotomy impossible to generalise for teaching;
- attempts to teach pitch movement overtly are likely to fail because of the subconscious level at which pitch operates;
- in the light of findings about intonation universals, some of the effort expended in teaching pitch movement seems in any case to be superfluous.

Turning to the issue of relevance, I discussed original data which suggest that non-use of English native-speaker-specific pitch movements does not affect intelligibility when English is used as a *lingua franca* between its non-native speakers. On the other hand, identifying and producing nuclear stress seem to be crucial for intelligibility when English is used in these international contexts. I demonstrated from my data a mismatch between learners' ability to recognise nuclear stress and their lack of ability to produce it. This leads to miscommunication because they expect nuclear stress to be appropriately placed and therefore have problems of understanding when it is not. However, the difficulty is relatively easy to sort out in the classroom: nuclear stress placement, whether unmarked (on the last content word of a word-group) or contrastive (somewhere else) is subject to clearly defined and thus teachable rules.

My conclusion is that while matters of pitch are best left for acquisition through natural exposure to English, nuclear stress can be both taught and learned in the classroom, and is essential for international intelligibility.

5.10 A critique of things lexical

Anthony Bruton, *University of Seville*

Both D Willis's *The Lexical Syllabus* and M Lewis's *The Lexical Approach* replace the structural syllabus with a lexical one, while being critical of alternatives. The critique of these two publications discloses some of their internal inconsistencies.

Willis argues that a specification of language based on word frequencies from a corpus can avoid the random selection of and exposure to language in communicative approaches. However, the actual practice reveals numerous qualifications on the original apparently scientific means of syllabus determination, apart from the fact that the basis of the whole proposal is the physical word.

Word frequency does not necessarily equate with utility, certainly not abroad, and different meanings of words have different frequencies. Frequency does not resolve selection as it produces some significant omissions – e.g. lexical sets and classroom items (p 77). The frequency levels are arbitrary and so is the weighting and sequencing within them. Frequency is therefore used to highlight (p vi/74). However, highlighting does not necessarily result in intake, and certainly not if the frequencies are based on adult native (written) language. Very often the most frequent items are the most ambiguous or polysemous, which does not facilitate their acquisition. Finally, texts and tasks are sequenced intuitively (p 76–77/85) and it is impossible to impose frequency levels on input without distorting it, which is something Willis criticises (p 45). Howcver it does not deter him from suggesting material recorded specially by native speakers and some modified texts (p 74). All in all, the initial scientific argument becomes progressively less and less credible as it progresses.

The Lexical Approach is a prescriptive crusade against grammatical syllabuses and PPP methodology, but it is so confusing for this reader that it is difficult to identify what the approach really is or to pinpoint what the real novelties are. The lexical part of the approach boils down to suggesting that lexical forms are more important than grammatical forms, that idiom is crucial, and that co-text is to be given precedence over context. Lewis rejects the PPP paradigm in favour of the *Observe-Hypothesise-Experiment* one, and joins the reception-first bandwagon, while failing to recognize that TPR is nothing more than stimulus→response in disguise, that context is critical to TPR, and that analysis, which he rejects (p 4/97/121), is fundamental to any hypothesis formation. In fact, Lewis draws on no research into lexical acquisition, particularly not studies showing that co-textual inferencing is usually highly unsuccessful in the short-term. Numerous other contradictions abound: criticisms of decontextualisation (p 81/106), while justifying it (p 116); suggesting diverse input and partial comprehension (p 27) alongside controlled listening (p 10); rejecting pattern practice (p 157) and recognising its benefits (p 159); rejecting PPP alongside the use of decontextualised drills (p 81); questioning the usefulness of rules (p 38), but then suggesting that students can be told rules (p 152) and that student formulated rules might be valid (p 150); proposing increased precision (p 121), while limiting the role of accuracy (p 158); suggesting fluency practice, while rejecting aspects of language use as habit; questioning language learning as the accumulation of items (p 107), while accepting the teaching of semantically dense items decontextually (p 110); and so on.

5.11 Three Walloons, six Japanese, two Italians, a Korean ... and a funeral

Tony Young, *Bell Language Trust*

This talk focused on one of the major challenges faced by EFL teachers operating in English-speaking countries: promoting spoken fluency in classes of diverse cultures.

Needs analysis usually (and unsurprisingly) reveals a positive hunger for *Speaking*, *Conversation*, *Saying the right thing* and the related point of *Being polite*. Teacher and class negotiate a syllabus allowing for a veto on topics a student does not want to look at (often *politics*). The negotiation is best carried out by the students completing a form, allowing time for consideration and helping to open up a channel of direct communication between less forthcoming students and the teacher.

With a similar aim, students keep a record card on which to write impressions of and reactions to activities. At the most basic level, students keep a record of their own talking time. Comments are also frequently made about embarrassments and misunderstandings which a teacher can clarify. A teacher can also add positive encouragements at any time.

Raising cross-cultural awareness is vital. Two useful lessons are *How to behave* and *What to say*. Picture prompts can be used showing, for example, people kissing and hugging, smoking in public places, queuing and eating 'on the hoof'. The aim here is to heighten awareness of differences in attitude, and to what extent these are purely personal or culturally informed. This can be drawn together with a look at *Good and Bad Manners in Britain*, an extract from a guide book, and a humorous text from *The Guardian* on how to behave in a pub. Students then act as consultants for others planning a visit to their country.

A study of polite forms in English is of great practical use and raises awareness of the idea of appropriacy. With high level students, the use of indirect questioning (*Do you happen to know...?*, *Would you mind...?*, etc.), as was pointed out by a member of the audience at the talk, usually causes great embarrassment to German and Swedish speakers and rings a lot of bells with Koreans and Japanese. Very nice activities in this area can be found in *In Advance* Unit 2 (Nelson), which draws on examples from Japanese society as well as focusing on embedded questioning in English. Japanese examples put Japanese students in the position of being knowers and thus help to raise their confidence and profile within the group.

It is important to isolate fillers when teaching conversation skills. Raise students' awareness of their use in their own first languages before looking at the likes of *Well*, *Anyway*, *I see*, etc. Similarly, students benefit from looking at reply questions and the use of question tags. A very good lesson covering these points is Unit 7 of the 'old' *Cambridge English Course* 3.

Conclusions

- business English text books give raising cross-cultural awareness a high priority, presumably in response to the commercial imperative of actually doing business, but it is still a neglected area in general English texts;

- task-based speaking activities give students the opportunity to achieve, helping to foster a sense of progress being made in spoken fluency;
- part of the wider role of the EFL profession is to broaden international understanding. The approaches mentioned above benefit learners of all nationalities. On a more mundane level, they help class dynamics and generate a better, more cooperative spirit among students.

5.12 'Shorts'

Doing pronunciation: A beginner's guide,
Bryan Jenner, Universität Wien

It is necessary to distinguish three broad groups of learners

- those who want to sound native-like: there are some, but they are probably a minority
- those who do not need to sound native-like
- those who do not want to sound native-like.

Those in the second and third categories need to be intelligible to each other but a native model is not strictly necessary. What they do need is a set of priorities and a minimal pronunciation kit.

... For learners who do want to sound native-like, we would also need to look at typical features of voice quality and setting as well as some additional vowel contrasts.

Cross-cultural misunderstanding: the importance of pragmatics, *Farid Aitsiselmi, University of Bradford*

One of the difficulties in understanding foreign discourse derives from a lack of knowledge about the cultural background in which the language is used. As they are more apparent, the errors made by learners of a foreign language due to transfers from their native phonology, lexicon or syntax are well documented and dealt with extensively in teaching materials as well as in foreign language classes. But the errors, misperceptions and misunderstandings which result from transfers from the schematic knowledge that learners bring with them into the classroom are generally ignored.

In fact, an essential component of language communication is neglected in foreign language teaching, namely the socio-cultural aspects of all utterances. Very little information (either formal or informal) is given to help learners develop their ability to understand underlying social meanings. It is assumed that they will acquire these aspects of communication as they learn the language. But this rarely happens. Students need guidance from teachers who, in turn, need to be prepared for this task.

Pronunciation in a lexical approach, *Jonathan Marks, Łeba, Poland*

In listening, identification of the phonological structure of the tone units is an essential part of processing auditory signals and interpreting them as part of larger message structures. Evidence of misreadings suggests that effective reading – silent reading – relies on the ability to segment a text as if it was being heard; skilled reading aloud makes this process explicit. Similarly, during the writing process, writers may find it useful to hear inwardly, or even read aloud, stretches of the text they are composing.

All this suggests a need and an opportunity to integrate knowledge of lexis and grammar, pronunciation and fluency, with suprasegmental aspects of pronunciation as an inherent component of language knowledge rather than a superimposed veneer.

English – from the inside out, a deconstructive approach, *Wayne G A Gallard, Escola Universitária del Maresme*

The problem is four-fold:

1 Current 'communicative' exercises are often contrived, built around overly-specialised vocabulary, and too are culturally-dependent.

2 The idiosyncrasies and 'exceptions' of English, which are some of the real strengths of the language, are often hidden away and avoided in most current coursebooks.

3 ELT is big business and everybody wants to sell the hottest new series. Few seem to point out that English can be taught with little textual material or whatever material may be available.

4 The British/American English dichotomy is irrelevant. It's the English- as – *lingua franca* – call it 'Eurospeak', 'Global English', etc. – that should take center stage. English as a tool for international communication, not as a mechanism for spreading cultural awareness.

What's not in the textbooks, *Gloria Gaston-Dwyer*

Think, for example, of the many things a simple *Oh* can mean. *Oh it's you again* (resignation); *Oh, Oh* (forgetfulness); *Oh, I'd love to* (delight); *Oh, no* (distress); *Oh?* (disbelief); *Ohh!* (realisation); etc. In these cases, it is the situation and the intonation that generally indicate the intention of the speaker. The point is that these sounds made by native speakers DO have meaning. As such, it is necessary for non-native speakers to be able to interpret them long before they have to worry about learning how and when to produce them.

Word partnerships in academic English, *Hugh Dellar, University of Westminster*

It is not enough, I feel, for EAP material to tell students that they need to be evaluating, exploring cause and effect, providing evidence, and so on. Students also need to be told which language is commonly used to perform such functions. Lexical hints added to students' writing can often be enough to prompt the undertaking of redrafting, and students can be encouraged to notice how these functions are performed in other texts, and to keep records of the lexis that is used to do this.

The design, compilation and exploitation of an EAP corpus, *Martha A Jones, University of Nottingham*

This inductive type of approach (see Carter and McCarthy, 1995) is based on the three I's *Illustration-Interaction-Induction*. For example, students are given authentic spoken data to analyse, such as common features of conversation and discussion used in different situations (Illustration). They then discuss with other students how these features are used (Interaction), and through well-informed discussion, it is hoped that the students will work out the usage rules (Induction).

6 CONFERENCE REVIEWS

6.1 The 31st Annual *IATEFL* Conference – Window to the World of EFL

Guo Jieke, *Foreign Languages Department, South China University of Technology, Guangzhou*

English has been taught in China for almost a hundred years and except for a short period after the liberation when the teaching of Russian was mandatory in all secondary and tertiary institutions, it has been and it still is the most popular foreign language in China today. The teaching of EFL in China has always been strongly influenced by teaching trends abroad, a case in point being the introduction of the communicative approach and the notional-functional syllabus in China in the early eighties and their inclusion in the National College English Syllabus promulgated by the State Education Commission in 1985. Therefore, teachers of English in China are extremely interested in developments in EFL abroad, and the annual **IATEFL** conference, being a truly international event and representative of the state of the art and future developments in the field of EFL, is an occasion by which teachers of English in China can feel the pulse of the signs and times of the EFL community all over the world.

The 31st annual **IATEFL** conference was eventful not only because of the wonderful weather in Brighton, but even more so because of the wide range of topics that were covered during the very short four days of the conference. As a delegate from China, I was very much interested in the following topics, which I think also have a bearing on the teaching of EFL in China.

How to improve classroom methodology and the time/efficiency ratio of English classes in tertiary institutions is a question of prime importance as the total number of hours spent in teaching English in universities and colleges throughout China has come dangerously close to the point of crowding out other important courses, even the students' majors, without at the same time producing commensurate results. Consequently, the give-and-take revolving around Michael Lewis's Lexical Approach was extremely interesting, considering the fact that the Lexical Approach could provide another option in the choice of classroom methodology in university classrooms here in China.

The presentations on testing have also provided much food for thought since the results of tests and exams are often used as a standard for evaluating the quality of teaching and learning, and their washback effect often decides what is taught and learned. With the opening up of China to the outside world and the corresponding increase in exchange between the various sections of the Chinese academic, business and industrial worlds and their foreign counterparts, the importance of being able to communicate orally in English has now become the order of the day for non-English majors in the key universities of China. Accordingly, the teaching and especially the testing of oral communication skills are now important points of focus, with such matters as inter-rater consistency in assessing spoken English being of immediate interest. Other topics such as the EFL item banking projects and writing for exams, which were also discussed during the panel on testing, are also of interest to the EFL community in Chinese universities.

Since English is taught in a setting in which students come into contact with it chiefly through the classroom, how to provide sufficient input that is both interactional and fun and which can be accessed by students whenever they feel like doing so is another topic that is of great interest to EFL teachers, especially those in the major cities and key universities of China. Computers are now quite common in China's universities and many university students and even middle school students in the wealthier coastal areas possess their own personal computers. Many undergraduate and postgraduate students in the key universities also have access to the Internet, so the panel discussions on the use of computers and the multimedia in the teaching of EFL has provided a lot of interesting and viable ideas and activities for making increased use of computers to provide guided and natural input and practice for individual learners.

Considering the sheer number of people from all walks of life studying English in China, the teaching of English in China is a big proposition. So it would not be surprising if I were to say that most of the topics discussed at the congress would not only be of interest to me, but also of interest to teachers of English at all levels in China. It is only with regret, as the Chinese saying goes *That I couldn't divide myself into several beings* and attend several sessions that I would have liked to attend at the same time.

If I was disappointed at all, it was that some of the plenaries did not fully live up to my expectations. Another *fly in the ointment*, as the English say, was that despite the fact that the various publishing houses and book centres put up interesting exhibitions of their latest books, many of the books exhibited were not available at the Brighton ELB stall. But on the whole, the 31st **IATEFL** conference is an event to remember, especially for some members of the Chinese delegation who were on their first visit to Britain, providing them with the opportunity to see and meet in person some of the big names in the world of EFL which were only familiar to them on the covers of the books they read back home in China, and giving all of us an opportunity to learn at first-hand of the new developments in TEFL.

6.2 My conference experience

Rama Mathew, *Central Institute of English and Foreign Languages, Hyderabad*

Conferences are too huge and bewildering. The **IATEFL** Conference was more so this year, although I had found my feet to some extent from last year's experience. I did however, have a feeling of excitement as I circled the talks I was interested in for the day. Too many in one session sometimes, but not always. I was glad to have some 'free' time on hand to look at the posters, again an interesting and attractive fare, the visuals giving the poster presenters a clear edge over the others. I also needed time to catch up on discussions with people whose talks I had found useful, interesting, relevant and so on. In fact I came to realise by the second day that I would be wise to cut down on the formal talks and make time to clarify issues that emerged from the talks, explore future possibilities of collaboration across the globe, and more importantly look carefully at the ELT Resources Exhibition, the bakery which sold hot cakes. I had to decide on what I could learn and take back with me to India. Honestly, this was not at all an easy task. In addition, I felt the heavy responsibility of being the *Ray Tongue Delegate*.

In this review, I am trying to collect all my experiences together – both formal and informal – to see where I stand at the end of the conference. Of the seventeen talks I participated in, including my own, I found that thirteen of them focused on themes that were right up my street. The talks, the informal chats with old and new friends, and the crash course I put myself through in the ELT exhibition all point to enormous possibilities of further work at individual, institutional and national levels. I see two major themes in the four days' intensive exposure: Testing and Action Research for Teacher Development.

Testing

A distinct feature of the talks given by Rex King and Peter May was the focus on public/final exams and their washback on teaching and on learning in the classroom. If 'teaching to the text' is a tradition that cannot easily be wiped out, the question *How can they be exploited to ensure good washback?* seems to be a crucial one – a very familiar situation, indeed. It is necessary to address this question from two angles: firstly, designing the exam with desirable washback as the guiding principle; and secondly, equipping the teacher to be able to handle the tests, i.e. the formats, content, appropriate level of difficulty vis-à-vis the teaching methodology in a way that is appropriate to the (communicative) test in question.

Peter May's tasks are a very good example of how students can be helped in the classroom not only to avoid traps in tests but also to deal with the metalanguage of testing that is necessary to be an efficient test taker. Further, the tasks stem from and feed back into tests, the ultimate goal of language learning in a practical sense, and provide for interesting classroom-based activities in simulated, interactive contexts. Language learning is an inevitable by-product of the entire exercise of test-preparation. Thus, the potential exams have of being an instrument of change is exploited.

The situation in India is one where, with a few exceptions, traditional content-based (as opposed to skill-based) exams override all other educational concerns. The discussion of the historical, political and cultural considerations that underlie such a tradition is not relevant here. For example, the changed exams of the Central Board of Secondary Education (CBSE) and the Maharashtra Board are to a large extent 'unseen'. Therefore the first important question we need to ask is, if Hong Kong and some Exam Boards in India can have exams that promote good language teaching-learning practices, why can't the others? Secondly, once a new exam is introduced, how is the change supported at the classroom level? The case of the CBSE gives some evidence of a negative washback where teachers 'coach' students for the exam through wrong means. This can be attributed largely to lack of (testing) awareness among teachers. The same story as in Hong Kong: it is comparatively easy to change the exams and text books, but it will take generations to change teaching methods. It seems that the core of all educational change is the question of training/education. I think we will also need to work more and more with individual learners' language as they work on a task in the classroom, as Andrew Harrison's project sets out to do. But in India, we need to reckon, more than anything else probably, with the problems of large numbers, be it in testing or teacher training. Therefore, the issue of feasibility and quality vs quantity looms large. The Brazilian experience (Rosa Lenzuen and Chris Palmer) provides some ideas for coping with large numbers and distances. We have a lot to learn from each other.

Action Research for Teacher Development

Another theme that drew my attention was action research by teachers. There were several presentations that focused on teacher research for on-going teacher development. Some of the issues that seem crucial in the area are:

- the social constructivist perspective for negotiating the practical and theoretical needs of teachers
- collaborative action research within a reflective approach for teacher development and learner autonomy
- problems in the application of academic research to practical EFL contexts, and therefore
- the issue of legitimising teacher research and the need for involving teachers in classroom centred research to sustain on-going curriculum renewal.

The secondary level curriculum project (known as the *CBSE-ELT Project*) that has been in progress in India has enabled academic experts and teachers to address issues in teacher education, teacher research, and curriculum renewal (including changes in exam scheme) collaboratively. The question that needs to be examined in action research projects however, is *What kind of teacher research is appropriate?* Action research so far has meant for the teacher an additional burden which he or she has to take on 'aside from' teaching. Therefore one comes across comments by teachers such as 'Not again, I don't have time', as Alan Maley also pointed out. I think we might need to look at teacher research as an approach and an attitude to everyday classroom work rather than an eight to ten step package that culminates in a report and, more crucially, in an 'action'. The tasks that were used for raising teachers' awareness of what classroom research involves (Barbara Thornton and Wasyl Cajkler) would be a very effective way of initiating teachers into research.

There were many other notions/ideas that need to be picked up and worked on further: portfolio assessment of teaching in pre- and in-service training, learning new activities that go beyond recipes to more generative tasks, issues in teacher recruitment and teacher training, the process approach to teacher training, evaluation of materials by teachers, and many others.

There were yet other areas that I found intellectually very stimulating but I don't know how I can immediately concretise in India: for example, the lexical approach and the associated problems. One reason for this is the local context itself, which defies some of the very challenging notions that are popular elsewhere. For example, the skill of supplementing and/or creating new materials in a context where books are centrally prescribed and exams are text-based is rather far-fetched for the Indian teacher. The other is a personal one. Needless to say, I have been constrained by my own limited competence and areas of interest and specialisation in choosing the sessions and making sense of them. Therefore, this review is not an 'objective' review of the entire conference.

Writing this review, if a bit sketchily, has helped me marshal my understanding and get a perspective on what might be some of the useful ways in which it can be consolidated in my own context. I think I could be a more perceptive reviewer if I were to do it another time.

6.3 Conference review

Janaina Cardoso, *Cultura Inglesa, Rio de Janeiro*

In her plenary paper *The English Teacher as a Professional*, Penny Ur points out that to be considered professionals, we English teachers have to be part of a community, to commit ourselves to reaching certain standards of performance, to publish, to learn, to be autonomous and to be responsible for training new teachers.

Hence, the *31st **IATEFL** Annual Conference* contributed remarkably to the development of the delegates as professionals. We teachers experienced the sense of belonging to an international community and had the chance of meeting people from all over the world and exchanging ideas and experiences. It is always comforting to discover that despite having very different realities, we all face very similar difficulties.

The Open Forums, for instance, represent an opportunity to meet teachers with similar interests and at the same time to be aware of what is going on in the SIGs. I participated in the Open Forums of my two main SIGs – *Learner Independence* and *Research*. In fact, I believe that all teachers should be more and more active in their SIGs.

For non-native teachers of English, the **IATEFL** conference also represents the possibility of presenting the studies they have been involved in. In this convention, the international representation was very significant. My country, for example, sent more than 25 delegates, most of whom presented papers or posters, or were involved with the association in a variety of ways. Moreover, the conference may also represent a chance to publish our studies, not only in the proceedings, but also in newsletters and sometimes in books (**IATEFL** publications, for example).

Particularly important to our development was the opportunity to learn. The conference allowed delegates to choose from a list of varied, interesting topics presented in hundreds of different sessions, six plenaries, and a number of poster presentations.

For the members of the *Learner Independence* SIG, the conference began on 1 April with the *LI SIG Pre-conference Symposium*, which was a success. Phil Riley opened the event with a polemical talk stressing the view of the teacher as counsellor. The discussion groups and the colloquia represented a big forum for discussion and analysis of the present roles of teachers and learners. The event closed with a panel discussion involving John Trim, Phil Riley, Eryl Griffiths, Susan Sheerin, Peter Wilby and George Blue.

Congratulations to Jenny Timmer for the organisation of the symposium – we look forward to other pre-conference events next year!

On 2 April, the annual conference was officially opened by the Chair, Madeleine du Vivier. The plenary session given by Jean Aitchison attracted so many delegates that the majority of them were unable to take part in it. Fortunately for the ones who missed it, there was the choice between the poster presentations and the resource exhibition.

In fact, the element of choice represented a very positive point and at the same time was a problem we had to face. A good example of this was the session on Thursday at 11:45. The delegates we had to choose between several interesting presentations, including sessions featuring Adrian Underhill, Philip Prowse, Michael Swan, Mario Rinvolucri.

Some of the highlights of the presentations I had the chance of attending were:

- Andrew Wright's relaxing and extremely useful demonstration on how to involve young learners (of all ages) in the production of stories.
- Aldo Higashi's talk on an innovative topic: Using Internet for communicative practice. He listed a number of interesting sites for teachers and learners, and suggested many creative 'net-activities'.
- Ingrid Freebairn and Chris Barker's presentation of their new book based on research with teenagers and teachers from different parts of the world. It was good to know that learners' and teachers' opinions are being taken into serious consideration.
- John Field's analysis of the implications of using authentic listening in the classroom and suggestions on how to deal with authenticity.
- Flavia Vieira's account of an in-service teacher development project being developed in Portugal, in which the autonomy given to teachers made them more aware of the importance of learner autonomy.
- Michael Hoey's plenary: by using the metaphor of a trip, he skilfully took us into the world of discourse.
- Michael Lewis started by defending the lexical approach brilliantly, and left a polemical question in the air: why do we non-native teachers, who share the same language as our learners, avoid the use of translation as a tool in the classroom?

Other presentations were equally relevant to our development, but it was impossible to be present at all of them.

Another remarkable opportunity we foreign teachers have when participating at **IATEFL** conventions is to meet and exchange ideas with researchers, linguists and other teachers who have been of great importance in the development of the teaching English in our countries. In this conference I had the pleasure of meeting Michael Swan and John Holmes in person!

The conference was a rewarding experience. The only thing I would like to add is that it would be wonderful to see more teachers (not only teacher trainers and managers) participating in it. Therefore, I would end with a thought for EFL top managers: Think how much your teachers will profit from participating in **IATEFL** conferences! Think how much your institutions will gain from having sponsored teachers who come back home much more motivated and enriched, both as people and as teachers! This is certainly an investment which will bring benefits for everyone.

To the conference organisers, congratulations on a good job! I hope to see you next year – if I find someone to sponsor my trip.